A Broken Candle

Still gives light

The Chuck Lewis Story

By Chuck Lewis

© 2018 Chuck Lewis

A Broken Candle Still Gives Light: The Chuck Lewis Story

Chuck Lewis Ministries, Inc.

PO Box 440113

Aurora, CO 80044

www.chucklewisministries.com

Lewis80044@yahoo.com

Words of Encouragement for Us ALL...

I wrote this book to bless you and to introduce you to my very best friend, Jesus. I believe you will be encouraged as you read my story. Some parts will make you laugh. Other parts will probably make you cry. Parts of my life were very painful; but you should know that God has turned that pain into joy.

What God has done for me, He can also do for you. Please pray this prayer as you start this book. "Father, thank You for Your love. Help me hear Your voice and see You as I read this book. I want to know You, Jesus, and the power of Your resurrection. Give me eyes to see You and ears to hear You today. In Jesus name, Amen."

For as long as I could remember, I wanted to see miracles. When I was six or seven years old, I went with my father to pray for a man with a knee problem. The man's knee was 2-3 times bigger than it should have been. My dad told me to watch the knee as he prayed. When he prayed, the knee went down to the right size so fast, it was like someone let all the air out of a balloon.

I want to make you a promise. If you read through this book and start to do what God says to do, you will see miracles around you very soon. God has not changed over the years and He still works miracles. His arm is not shortened and His power has not weakened at all.

God is the same yesterday, today, and tomorrow. He has not

changed. His miracle working power is available to you today!

God the Father loves to pour out His love on us. He loves to heal us of our physical and emotional problems. The Holy Spirit loves to draw us close and explain things to us in a way we can understand. He loves to give us information and words of knowledge about the circumstances we are in and the people with whom we are dealing. Jesus loves to walk with us everywhere we go and He loves to help us with everything we do. He promised to be with us always, no matter where we have to go.

Matthew 28:20 says, *"I am with you always, even to the end of the age."* If it's one thing I know, it's that Jesus keeps His promises.

In this book, I've included some verses from the Bible. When you come across a verse, take some time to mull it over. Ask the Holy Spirit to help you understand what the verse means. The Holy Spirit will teach you as you meditate on the verse. You will start to change as you begin to get revelation and insight about what God says in His Word. When you start to do what God says to do, things in your life will change even faster.

One word from God can change your life. I have included some of the life skills I learned from God as I tell my story in this book. These life skills will help you hear God more clearly and they can transform your life. I think one of the reasons God had me become a counselor was that I needed to learn these life skills. I had a lot of things wrong with me and I needed more help than most people. Every time I share these skills with other people, I get more understanding about them and about me.

One word from God can change your life!

As you notice a skill mentioned in the book, ask the Holy Spirit to meet with you and teach you about how that life skill can help you. Learning about the foundational life skills I mention in my story will help you to live a more successful life.

The life skills are rooted in common sense. To be honest, they are pretty ordinary. Because they are skills and not talents people are born with, you can learn them. It does take practice to use these skills well.

God used these principles and strategies to help me learn how to walk in wisdom. Some of them have to do with how I interact with other people and some of them have to do with how I personally grow into maturity. Some of the deepest revelations God has taught me have to do with confronting the lies I believed about myself and replacing them with God's truth about who I truly am.

That life skill which I call cognitive distortions, had very little to do with anyone else in my life. It had everything to do with how I thought and how to set the lies aside and put the truth in their place. So much freedom is available to us when we choose to embrace the truth.

So much freedom is available to us when we choose to embrace the truth.

Jesus said in **John 8:32**, *"And you will know the truth and the truth will set your free."*

One of the most powerful communication skills I've learned, for example, has to do with listening to the other person in a conversation and making sure I understand what they are saying before I respond. That life skill, the speaker/listener technique, has made a positive impact on every relationship in my life.

Thank You...

I've wanted to write out my story for many years because I knew it would help other people. Recently, the Lord has brought some people into my life to help me complete this project.

First of all, thank you to all the people who sent funds so we could have the first batch of books printed.

Thank you, John Carvey, for your help with most of the writing.

Thank you, Beatrice Bruno, The Write Drill Sergeant, for editing and publishing.

I also want to thank you, Barbara, my loving wife of 24 years. You have been a steady and deep source of love and encouragement for me. I would not be who I am today if you were not in my life. Thank you for encouraging me to put my story on paper.

Most of all, Thank You, Jesus! Thank You for loving me and paying the price on the Cross so I could be part of Your family forever. Introducing other people to You is my great joy.

A Broken Candle: The Chuck Lewis Story

Foreword

My heart swells with happiness as I take pen to paper in honor of the publication of *A Broken Candle Still Gives Light.* First, however, I want to tell you how I have come to write the foreword to it. Hopefully, you will see why I am tempted to suggest that you skip the foreword and rush headlong into the story.

Here is what happened. Pastor Chuck Lewis introduced me to God! In truth, my appointment with Pastor Chuck became my introduction to the true and living God. The sudden death of the younger of my two daughters had devastated me. I was stumbling through the movements of grief and loss – Shock, Denial, Anger, Bargaining, Acceptance – falling down much of that time. I was stuck. Mired in pain that paralyzed me, I struggled just to crawl out of the bed in the morning or midafternoon or even at dinner, and crawl back in an hour or two later. I didn't care about too much of anything, but I had been socialized in a culture of politeness; thus, I felt obligated to "go through the motions" of civility.

Off to Pastor Chuck I went for weekly sessions. He carefully tended to the condition of my soul and spirit. No, he didn't say, "Now Dorothie, I'm going to introduce you to God and everything's going to be alright," he didn't offer a "balm from Gilead." He didn't minimize or sugar coat my sadness, anger, aloofness. No, he simply met me as a brother, whose life mirrored mine in many ways while they were as different as night from day in others. More than anything, the centerpiece of Pastor Chuck's ministry continues to be the "Word." He speaks the God-breathed Word out of his belly, effortlessly and purely. He introduced me to a Personal Father, through illustrations, anecdotes, explanations, questions, and other creative methodologies.

Between the ages of eight and sixteen, Chuck might have read or heard **Jeremiah 29:11** read aloud. Did Chuck read this scripture and tuck its promise within his heart? Did he hide it in the corner of his mind?

"For I know the plans I have for you," declares the Lord, "plans to prosper you and not to harm you, plans to give you a hope and a future."

Perhaps Chuck does not remember when his "Perfect Storm" happened, when he was compelled to answer the Call from the Almighty; recognized that our Father makes no mistakes in any aspect of our lives; and accepted his assignment to serve. God has been teaching Pastor Chuck in myriad ways for many decades, identifying the wide range of needs His children encounter and knowing how great Pastor Chuck's impact would be.

For the first sixteen years of his life, Pastor Chuck's world measured a mere 9' x 12', the size of a small bedroom. He rarely ventured outside that space, his brothers having painted a gruesome picture of a dangerous world that frightened him. The day after Pastor's encounter with God, the Holy Spirit opened the doors of his mind, as far as it could stretch; released his physically entrapped body, and populated him with gifts and skills, situations and challenges, courage and personality, and choices and ideas that the men and women who would be assigned to him would need.

The faithfulness of God rescued Pastor Chuck from the loneliness, isolation, and pain of a dysfunctional family and equipped Chuck to help others who have suffered disrespect, degradation, indignity, low self-esteem, and shaky self-image along with the numerous outrages of the human condition.

I want you to read about this extraordinary journey into the life of an indomitable, tenacious Man of God. Uncanny, the nature and condition of Pastor Chuck's birth reflects the prophecy God wrote about Jeremiah: *"Before I formed you in the womb, I knew you. Before you were born, I set you apart…"* **Jeremiah 1:5a**.

Let me share with you, if you would, why God ordained Chuck to write his story which rivals the Charles Dickens' novels about boys growing up in 18th Century England. Though not legally orphaned, Chuck might well have been. He felt unwanted and unloved by his birth family, he withdrew into the shelter of powerful arms that neither left nor forsook him. I give you now, *A Broken Candle Still Gives Light.*

Dr. Dorothie Clark, Grief Education Counselor
Author/Speaker

Chapter 1 - A Hard Beginning

I was a breech baby, coming out feet-first instead of head-first. I was born in 1951 and the instruments and methods doctors used to help mothers deliver breech babies were not as good as they are today. When the doctors turned me around inside my mother, so I would have a better chance of survival, they hit my head on my mother's pelvic bone and it injured my spine. That injury caused extensive bruises on the side of my face. The forceps caught my right eye, nearly pulling it out of the socket, and my top lip was severely busted open. My throat was paralyzed so I couldn't make a sound. They didn't think I would live; and if I did, they were sure I would never be normal.

In a normal birthing process, the baby turns around so the head is down and ready to enter the birth canal. Breech babies don't get into position. If they are not manually moved inside the womb, it makes the birthing process much more difficult.

Years after my birth, I was at the altar praying at a church meeting and the pastor had a Word of Knowledge for me. He told me I was born breech because I didn't want to be born. He said there was a spirit of rejection on me that went back seven generations.

My birth was a good news, bad news situation. The good news was that they were able to turn me around inside my mother's womb so I could be born naturally. The bad news was that they injured my spine and caused a lot of other damage as they turned me. The discoloration and bruising I had at birth were extensive. The birthmarks I was left with were permanent.

Also, when I was older, I found out how difficult my birth was. I remember thinking, "They must have put 'Reject' on my basket in the nursery."

As I grew up, I didn't think God would want someone like me. I couldn't imagine that He would love me. How on earth could God love someone who had so many problems?

I was also a blue baby at birth. I didn't get enough oxygen because the umbilical cord was wrapped around my neck. The lack of oxygen was severe enough to cause me to develop cerebral palsy. Often, a baby will not get enough oxygen when there are complications in the birthing process. The length of time a baby goes without air determines the extent of the damage that happens to the baby's body. I'm sure the doctors did the best they could, but it takes time to turn a baby around inside the womb. Each second could be the difference between life or death.

Most of the time when you see someone with cerebral palsy, they're in a wheelchair and can't walk. People with cerebral palsy often have severe brain damage. I am thankful I didn't go without oxygen for very long. Although I did not develop brain damage, it did affect my upper body. I had uncontrollable tremors and involuntary movements of my upper torso, making it very difficult for me to feed myself or even put on my own clothes, especially buttoning my shirts.

The doctors said that even though I made it through the critical parts of my birth, I would never be able to do much. They painted a grim picture to my parents and told them I would live the life of an invalid and other people would have to take care of me. Now, I love doctors! I think medical science is amazing. But doctors are simply operating according to what they know from a scientific and medical perspective. They don't want to give people false hope, so they focus on the facts as the medical community understands them. But God...

"But God" is one of my favorite phrases. I am so glad my parents knew God and they prayed for my healing. I am so glad God intervened in my life. The medical news about me was bad and science did not have a solution. "But God" did have a solution and I am living proof that God still works miracles today.

There are so many reasons I shouldn't be doing what I'm doing right now. Just because something looks impossible doesn't mean it is. As you read my story, it could be the beginning of a brand new story and future for you. I know God has a good plan for your life no matter where you are right now.

My parents believed the Word of God. They also believed in the power of God to heal me; and so, they began to pray. By the time I was five months old, the Lord miraculously healed the purple discoloration, birthmarks, and bruises on the side of my face and neck; my eye that was almost out of the socket from the birth trauma became normal; my top lip that was severely busted open was healed; and, my throat was not paralyzed anymore.

As I grew, I developed a triple curvature of the spine. My spine ran like an "s" up and down my back. My body didn't look or respond like other people's bodies and I developed an inferiority complex. Despite all the physical miracles God had done so far in my life, I still felt inferior. It was so bad, I was afraid to talk to anyone.

I lived my life in my bedroom and wouldn't even eat with my own family. My mother would fix a plate and bring it into my bedroom so I could eat alone. I was embarrassed to even eat with my family because they criticized my involuntary movements. It was easier to eat alone than to face that kind of rejection.

I felt very unsafe. I wanted to have my family's acceptance and support but they didn't know how to give it to me. I developed a lot of self-hatred. I felt so unsafe in my own home that I didn't even want to use the bathroom. Because I had to walk through the living room to get to the bathroom, that meant I had to pass my brothers or my mom and dad to get there. I would hold it in for as long as I could. It seemed like every time I went through the living room, I got yelled at.

"Stop shaking like that!"

"Quit holding your head like that!"

"Quit shaking your head!"

"Quit walking like that!"

I was angry, sad, lonely, and confused.

"What did I do?"

I had no answers. There was no one in my life at that time who could coach me.

I would have loved to have been able to control those physical manifestations of cerebral palsy, but I could not. My physical condition and the problems I had as a result of cerebral palsy carried over to every other area of my life. I didn't realize that who I am is different than what I look like or what my body did on an involuntary basis.

Who you are… your value and worth… are not what you look like or what your body does or does not do. It's based on what God says about you. He created you and loves you deeply.

When I was fifteen or so, I fantasized that my family was not really the people in the house with me. My real family loved me and interacted with me in a supportive and kind way. We traveled around the world helping people by preaching the gospel and teaching them life skills. They would be coming for me any day now, walking up to the door and informing my parents that there was a mistake at the hospital. I had to leave with them so I could live with my real family.

I lived that way for the first sixteen years of my life. My parents loved God and prayed effectively for some aspects of my physical healing. Unfortunately, they didn't know how to help me emotionally. They thought yelling at me would help me. They thought I could control the involuntary movements if I really wanted to. Needless to say, I could not control the movements. The only way I could deal with my emotional pain was to isolate myself in my room.

I went to public school until I was ten. During those years, I focused on making as little human contact as possible. At school, I was teased and made fun of by other kids. I discovered during this time that kids can be mean because they don't understand what's going on for the other person. They just see that they are different and so they tease them. Every day after school, I went right back to my room. It was so hard for me to learn in that environment. I was so focused on the negative things the other kids said to me and how badly they treated me, that I couldn't concentrate on what the teacher was trying to teach.

I remember one event when I was about 10 years old that surprised me. My mom and dad had an argument and I saw mom in the living room crying softly. When I asked her what happened, she said, "Your dad and I had words and he said some things that hurt my feelings."

Dad was already in bed.

At the age of 10, I really took a risk and woke him up and said, "Hey dad, mom's really struggling out here and needs to talk about what you said. I need you to get up and talk with her."

My dad was so strong in his personality. Part of me thought he could have really hurt me for confronting him like that. He could have easily taken me out to the woods and you would have never seen me again. Instead, he got up out of bed and came out to where Mom was. I said, "Mom's really hurting, you need to tell her you're sorry." And he did.

"Mom, do you forgive him?" I asked.

I didn't know it at the time, but God had given me a gift. That gift worked even when I didn't know how to use it very well. My parents didn't know how to develop my gift of counseling, **but the Holy Spirit did.**

In Junior High, I went to a special school for the physically handicapped. My dad drove me there every day on his way to work and then picked me up after work.

I remember thinking, "Why do I have to go here? I don't have problems like these other kids!"

Most of the kids in my special class were in wheelchairs and had some serious issues. "Certainly, I'm not as bad off as these guys!" I remember thinking.

At some level, my brain didn't understand that I had a physical handicap that kept me from being able to learn in a normal school setting. Because of the involuntary upper body movements, one of the problems I had was that I could not write very well. Other people could not read what I was trying to write. To be honest, there were times I couldn't make it out either. It was like I was writing in another language but there wasn't an interpreter.

Another reason my parents and I decided I should go to the special school was that kids in the normal school setting teased me and made fun of me all the time. They were brutal. It felt like all the kids, even the nice ones, were bullies when it came to me.

After I became a counselor, I met a third grade teacher in the Denver school system. He told me that he had one class of third graders that confronted the bully in the school successfully. Twenty-three of the kids had been together since

Kindergarten and had learned to stick up for and to protect each other. When they talked to the bully on the playground, they told him that teasing and pushing were not acceptable.

They went on to say, "We want you to be our friend and part of our group because you're funny and pretty cool. But you can't be part of our group if you're mean."

The bully stopped his mean behavior. He wanted to be liked by this group of kids, so he followed their rules. Although there were thirty-eight students in that class, they were the easiest class to teach because the core group of kids wanted to behave and learn.

If the kids in my class had been like that, I could have learned in the regular classroom. Often, all it takes is one or two people in a crowd to stand up and say, "Hey, that's not how we treat people" for the bully to back down.

My brothers and I helped dad with his construction projects during the summer. Sometimes, he would take us to Luby's cafeteria. I never went inside because I was too afraid of what people might think about me. Instead, my dad would bring a sandwich to me to eat in the truck while they ate inside. I remember one time asking my brothers what it was like to eat in the restaurant with Dad. They would often tease me and tell me stories just to increase my fear. My brothers told me the cafeteria had a buffet line and that you had to hold your tray in one hand and serve yourself food with the other hand. That was something I couldn't do because my hands shook so much. Then they told me that often after you had your tray full, you had to walk through the whole restaurant in order to find your table and everyone would watch you eat. That was way out of my comfort zone. I still had trouble walking at times. To carry a tray with food and a drink on it sounded like juggling chainsaws to me. **Impossible**!

They weren't trying to protect me; they weren't trying to help me get through a hard situation. They were trying to turn my fear into terror.

Another time, I remember going to the mall with my brothers. They made me walk about ten feet ahead of them. I asked them why. They said, "We're ashamed to be with you, we don't want people to know you're with us."

They were embarrassed by how I looked and my involuntary movements. I didn't get mad at them. I didn't demand to be treated with love and respect. They were my older brothers; what they said must be true. I must have been as embarrassing as they said I was. Those wounds ran deep. I formed a very poor self-image as a result of those kinds of events. I felt alone, unloved, and unworthy of being treated well by other people.

I met a Christian therapist after I started college. He spoke at a youth meeting at the church I was attending. Because his fees were so high, I knew I couldn't afford to see him. But, I also knew I really needed and wanted him to counsel me. I asked him if he would agree to see me and told him I didn't have any money. He asked God if he was supposed to help me and God said, "Yes." God is so good! He met with me for free for one and a half years after that. What a blessing he was in my life!

When I told him about the experience with my brothers, he said that Jesus spoke to him while I was talking. He told me that Jesus was there when I felt like I was walking alone; He was walking right beside me. Jesus was proud to be walking beside me. That brought so much healing to me to realize that Jesus was proud of me. The picture of Jesus entering into those moments when I was deeply wounded has continued to be a powerful source of encouragement in my life.

That image of Jesus walking beside me and Jesus being proud of me came to mind whenever I thought about those hard times from my past. I felt empowered by Jesus' love and presence. My confidence also increased as I realized Jesus would never leave me or forsake me.

In Matthew 28:20, Jesus says, "I am with you always, even to the end of the age." That's good news!

After I finished college, I had a dream that also helped me tremendously. In my dream, I was walking down the sidewalk in front of our house with Jesus and we stopped at my house and went in. I saw myself at five years old standing in the middle of my family in our kitchen. They were saying mean things to me and I had to just stand there and take it. I was a mess but no one was stepping up to defend me. Jesus and I broke through the crowd. We took the hands of the little boy and took him out of the house.

Jesus said, "You will never have to go through that abuse again."

It was so powerful for me to see Jesus and the adult version of me walking that 5 year old child version of me out of a dangerous and harmful situation. God's purpose is for us to grow up into maturity. That means we need to look at things from His perspective. **There is no abusive or mean behavior that God approves.**

This dream was another paradigm shift for me just like Jesus walking beside me in the mall. We are valuable as people. That's a law of God. Even people who don't know God but still follow His laws receive the benefits of agreeing with God. God downloaded in my spirit that I was way too valuable to be treated like that.

If you don't understand that you have value, you can't set appropriate boundaries. If you don't have appropriate boundaries set in place in your life, you will operate in a maladaptive way. Maladaptive means abnormal and unhealthy.

When we live with unhealthy beliefs and behaviors, we develop a lot of cognitive distortions.

I shared this message at a women's shelter. The director told me to be aware that some of the women may get up and walk out during the presentation. The shelter does not require that they stay and listen to someone talking if it isn't what they want to hear. It's one of the ways the shelter empowers the women to take control of their environment.

As I began to share with them about how valuable they are and that they do not deserve to be treated the way they were treated, all eyes were on me. They had never heard anything like that before. I could see some tears forming. After a few minutes, a number of the women were crying out loud. No one left the room. The Holy Spirit healed a number of the women at that meeting. The power of the Holy Spirit was very evident that night.

A number of years later, I was in the food court at Park Meadows Mall here in Denver. I saw a family eating lunch with their son who had cerebral palsy. The whole family was taking turns giving him a bite of food or a sip of soda. They were all talking together and he was a part of the conversation. They were all laughing and enjoying each other's company so much. I went over to talk to them and told them how impressed I was seeing them enjoying each other as a family. I told them how blessed their son was to be in their family. I'll never forget their response.

"Oh, we are so blessed to have him in our family. We can't imagine what our family would be like if he wasn't here. He is such an amazing young man."

When I saw their son beam at the words, I knew the family had told me the truth. That's what a functional family looks like. _Honor and respect are foundational elements of a functional family.

Another truth I learned is that different is not deficient. Just because someone is different does not mean they are deficient or missing something important to have as a person. Each one of us is divinely formed and created by God. God does not make junk. Psalms 139 gives a great picture of how God sees each one of us. Take a minute to read it in Appendix E. Let's pray...

Father, thank You that You never change. Your love for me and for each person reading this book has been constant and strong since before we were born. You knit each of us together when we were still in our mother's wombs and there is no person or power or circumstance that can keep us from Your love. And thank You that You are inviting every one of us to be part of Your functional family. In the name of Jesus Christ, Amen.

Chapter 2 - Beginning Again

If you're skeptical about miracles, I want you to pray a simple prayer right now.

"Okay, Father, I'm going to set this skepticism aside, Lord, and I will try to believe You."

In **Psalms 34:8**, David says, *"Taste and see that the Lord is good."* God doesn't need us to understand everything perfectly before we receive from Him the healing that we need. I've shared a lot of miracles just in the first chapter of this book. Honestly, that's just the tip of the iceberg. Make a decision to set your skepticism aside and believe what God says.

When I was sixteen years old, my father invited me to a Full Gospel Businessmen's Convention in downtown Denver. Although I was paralyzed by my shyness, I reluctantly went with him. My dad thought I had received the Lord a long time ago, but I hadn't. I only had enough of God in me to bug me, and not enough to bless me.

Thankfully, God knew exactly where my heart was. He knew how much I needed Him in my life. When the speaker gave the invitation to receive Christ, I went down to the front of the auditorium. My knees were shaking and it wasn't from the cerebral palsy. What was I doing? I was scared to come out of my room and here I was walking down to the front of a room with thousands of people watching! As it turned out, I was not alone. A lot of other people came forward to accept Jesus at that meeting.

I remember standing at the front of that Hilton Hotel ballroom saying, "Lord, I don't know why You would want a crippled-up mess like me."

I felt like a big mistake with buttons and zippers. I was intimidated by people because of my physical problems. I got tired of people staring at me and that made me withdraw. The feelings of inadequacy kept me isolated. I felt trapped in a body that wouldn't cooperate and I couldn't do anything about it. Have you ever felt that way? Even though I felt that way, I said, "Lord I give You my life, and I ask You to come into my heart. Live in me and take control of my life."

Now, it's one thing to hear about God. It's quite another thing to receive Him in your heart and your life. For years I had heard my parents talk about God and pray to Him but I wasn't so sure about what my parents said sometimes. I had gotten really good at keeping people at a distance because they seemed to hurt me so badly. It was really pretty easy to keep God at a distance, too...until that moment.

I had had a lot of misunderstandings and cognitive distortions about God. I was like a lot of other people who believe that if they just go to church, they will be saved. Well, that doesn't make much sense if you think about it.

Just because a cat has kittens in an oven, it doesn't make them biscuits, right? You can't be transformed into something just by going to a certain place. A lot of people going to church are not really Christians. There are a lot of people who go to church and sing about a heaven they will never see.

You could attend church on a regular basis all your life and not know Jesus personally. So it's important to ask Jesus Christ to come into your heart. That's what I did that night. I asked Jesus to come into my heart. When I did, I felt a power come into me like I'd never felt before.

Romans 10:9 says, "*If you openly declare that Jesus is Lord and believe in your heart that God raised him from the dead, you will be saved.*" Well, I confessed Jesus as my Lord that night and I believed that God raised Him from the dead. I knew something happened inside me because I felt a confidence I had never felt before.

Romans 10:9 If you openly declare that Jesus is Lord and believe in your heart That God raised him from the dead, you WILL be saved.

Before that night, I had lived my whole life isolated in my bedroom, hardly speaking to anyone. Even when supportive, loving people would come to my parents' home to visit, I'd go into my room until they left. I didn't know any other way to live. But when Jesus came into my heart, I felt like He walked into my room with me. My room was where I had isolated myself. No one ever came in. It was the only place I felt even a little bit safe and I never asked anyone to come in.

If you will ask Jesus into your heart, He will go with you everywhere you have to go. Honestly, there isn't anything that scares Jesus. When He is walking with you, you can walk in peace and confidence no matter what is going on around you. Well, that's exactly what happened in my spirit. I didn't see any changes happen to my physical body, but I felt something happen on the inside of me.

Going home from that convention, I began to talk to my father about what had just happened and how wonderful it was to receive Christ. My dad began to worship and praise the Lord in the pickup. I began to do the same. Pretty soon, my dad reached over and put one hand on me. As he drove, he prayed for me to be filled with the power of the Holy Spirit. I didn't know much about what my dad was praying for. That night, I received the Baptism of the Holy Spirit. It was amazing! This gift gave me the power to emotionally come out of my room.

Emotionally, I had felt like I was an amputee who had lost both legs. When the power of God came on me through the Holy Spirit, it was like two legs grew out from those old stumps. I felt like I was sitting in an emotional wheelchair and I was physically a basket case. I wanted to run in the race of life but couldn't. The Holy Spirit gave me legs when I received my prayer language. It became a new way of deepening my relationship to God, and, for those of you that have experienced it, I'm sure you have felt the same.

Monday morning when I woke up, I felt like a new person. In **2 Corinthians 5:17**, the Bible says, *"This means that anyone who belongs to Christ has become a new person. The old life is gone; a new life has begun!"*

I felt the same confidence David must have felt when he stood before Goliath. It was incredible! I had never experienced that in my life. I had lived an intimidated, shy, fearful life for as long as I could remember. I didn't know what it was like to be confident.

As I look back on that scene, I realize the Holy Spirit was prompting me to say what I said that morning. When I woke up, I felt the presence of the Holy Spirit. As soon as I put my feet on the ground, I said, "Satan, I have run from you in fear and intimidation all my life. I have hidden myself from people because I was embarrassed. I have hidden behind curtains and ducked out of rooms when I saw other people coming because I didn't want to face them. **But now, the Holy Spirit of God is in me and you're going to run from me for a change! I'm a new creation in Jesus Christ! Amen."**

I am a new creation in Christ! Amen

I felt a righteous indignation about how the enemy had ripped me off for so many years. I was determined not to let that continue.

For the first time in my life, I declared war on the enemy. Previously, I had felt so bad about myself, I had taped a piece of cardboard on the mirror in my bedroom so all I could see was my hair. I knew I needed to comb my hair, so I left that part of the mirror usable. But that was the only part of me I wanted to see. I got up and walked to the mirror and ripped the cardboard off. I didn't really know what I was doing. Later on, I realized that what I did that morning was a powerful strategy you can use to change your life.

When I said, "I am a new creation in Christ," I was taking a promise from the Bible that the Holy Spirit brought to mind. When I tore the cardboard off the mirror, I was confirming that the promise was true. When I said, "I'm a new creature in Jesus Christ," I used my mouth to agree with God and declared that what God said was true. I experienced firsthand what that verse said. My world changed because of that scripture. That truth became so real to me at that moment.

When you agree with what God says, it's like signing your name at the bottom of a contract that God wrote. God will take responsibility for completing His side of the contract. You know what your part is? Say "Yes" to God. Say "Amen," or "So be it," to what God says.

Jesus said in **John 8:32**, *"And you will know the truth and the truth will set you free."* Lies had chained me up my entire life. I had believed lies about myself, lies about God, lies about how the world worked, and lies about how God looked at me. I declared war on the enemy by exposing one of his lies and replacing it with God's truth. That night at the conference when I made Jesus the Lord of my life, my emotional healing began.

I felt more changes start to happen inside of me. **Isaiah 53:4-5** says, *"Surely He has borne our griefs—sickness, weakness, and distress—and carried our sorrows and pain. Yet we ignorantly considered Him stricken, smitten and afflicted by God. But He was wounded for our transgressions. He was bruised for our guilt and iniquities; the chastisement needful to obtain peace and well-being for us was upon Him, and by the stripes that wounded Him we are healed and made whole."*

It's with His stripes that we are healed. You don't have to earn it! The healing power of God began to work inside of me. As time went by, that healing power worked its way out so that my body also started to get well. I was crippled outside, but I was also very crippled inside. There are many people who look just fine physically. Inside, they're not fine at all. A lot of people feel very intimidated and bound by fear, grief, and guilt.

The Bible says that we have to believe if we want to receive anything from God. **Hebrews 11:6** states, *"And it is impossible to please God without faith. Anyone who wants to come to him must believe that God exists and that he rewards those who sincerely seek him."* The world and our natural minds say, "If I see it, then I'll believe it." You know what faith says? Faith says, "If you believe it, then you'll see it."

That first Monday after I got saved, I went to work with my dad on his construction job. At lunch, he asked me how many sandwiches I wanted from the restaurant. Up until this point, I was still eating in the truck because I didn't think I could get through the food line without making a huge mess.

I said, "Dad, I don't want any more sandwiches. I'm going to eat in that restaurant with you today."

The power of God was flowing through me and I carried my food on a tray to the table. For the first time in my life, at sixteen years old, I had lunch with my dad in a restaurant. We cried all the way through that meal. From the very first day that I accepted Jesus, I saw proof that I was a new creation in Christ. It was a miracle for me to be able to eat at the restaurant. I was saved on Saturday night; all day Sunday, I worshiped God; I ate in the restaurant with my dad on Monday. What a difference a day makes!

One day, years later, I was asked to open in prayer for a Special Olympics Banquet. I thought it would be a small room of people and not that big of a deal. When I got there, I found out that all the meeting halls were packed out and hundreds of people, the press, the Governor, and Miss America were there. My first thought was, "Turn around and go home! Just call them and say you're not feeling well and can't come."

It would have been sort of true because, when I saw all those people, I did feel sick. Then I remembered that Jesus was with me. He would stay with me every step of the way. He would be right there helping me when I prayed. I went into that room instead of running away. It was a great time! They even gave me an award for helping them with the event.

Years later, I shared my testimony at a church in Nebraska. After the meeting, one of the moms who attended sent me a letter. She said that her son attended the meeting and he had cerebral palsy.

"He was glued to you as you were speaking and it was as if every word you spoke went right into his spirit. Usually he squirms around at church and can't sit still for more than a few minutes at a time, but when he listened to you speak he was very still. As we were driving home my son said, "Mom, I have hope." He is fifteen and he had never told me that before."

That letter encouraged me so much! You never know how much impact your story will have to help someone else. All I could do was take one step of faith at a time. Actually, I didn't know how I could stand in front of all those people...much less pray to open the banquet. Courage is simply taking the next step God asks you to take in your life.

At sixteen years old, I experienced a powerful encounter with Jesus and I walked in a new, divine confidence for the first time in my life. But as with many things, we grow slowly. We take every journey one step at a time. God is still teaching me and helping me to walk in wisdom and freedom today. Growing up to be mature in Christ is a process, and I am so glad Jesus walks with us each step of the way. I ask God to give me favor all the time and so can you!

Prayer...

Father, please give me favor with You and with everyone I meet. Thank You for Your love. Help me to receive Your love deep into my heart. Give me the confidence to do what I don't feel I can. In the name of Jesus Christ, Amen.

Chapter 3 - College

Two weeks after I got saved, I stayed with some friends up in the mountains. These people were so good to me. I liked to think of them as my adopted parents. As I lay in my bedroom one night, I began to worship the Lord. It was dark and everybody had already gone to bed. You know, it really gets dark in the mountains. On this night, there was no moon at all.

I remember putting my hand in front of my face and thinking, "I can't even see my hand!" I began to worship the Lord. All of a sudden, I saw light coming from the bottom of the door.

I thought, "Is somebody out in the hall?" But then I realized the light was not at the very bottom of the door. It was really coming from the middle of the door towards the bottom. This light began to come in. I was a little bit afraid at first; but all of a sudden, I started feeling this peace, a wonderful, glorious peace.

As I continued to worship and praise the Lord, this light became bigger and bigger. Pretty soon, it formed into a person right by my bed. All of a sudden, this angelic being began to speak and welcomed me into the Kingdom of God. As he talked, I realized it was Jesus Who came to visit me. He told me that I had been called from birth to preach the Gospel.

Isaiah 61:1 says, *"The Spirit of the Sovereign LORD is upon me, for the LORD has anointed me to bring good news to the* *poor. He has sent me to comfort the brokenhearted and to proclaim that captives will be released and prisoners will be freed."*

Jesus said that I had been called from birth to preach the Gospel and to do exactly what this Scripture said to do. He was also there to welcome me into the Kingdom of God. I thought that was glorious and I worshiped the Lord.

I was so excited, I didn't want to go to sleep. I wanted to just keep talking to Jesus. I fell asleep anyway because the peace of God was so strong in the room. I got up the next morning and was sitting at the breakfast table with my adopted parents.

I remember saying, "Oh, isn't it glorious when you get saved, and Jesus appears to you and welcomes you into the Kingdom? What was that like for you guys?"

Well, they looked at me like a horse looking at a new gate.

"What are you talking about?" they said.

"Well, you know," I responded, "When Jesus appears to you and welcomes you into the Kingdom of God. I mean, that's just incredible!"

They said, "That never happened to us."

I said, "Really? Well, I thought it happened to everybody."

I knew that what Jesus said was the truth and that I needed to prepare myself to do what God had just told me I would be doing for the rest of my life. I had to go to Bible College. He told me to prepare for full-time ministry, and as I went, He would heal me.

Actually, my parents didn't believe I could get through college. They purchased a small motel because they thought it would be a business I could run even if I had multiple physical and emotional problems. After I got saved, I started paying attention in school in a new way. I could understand what was being taught because I wasn't preoccupied with my problems. My new confidence allowed me to concentrate and learn in the classroom so that going to college became a possibility.

My dad was the International Director of the Full Gospel Businessmen's Fellowship for about fifteen years. One month after I accepted Jesus, I was speaking at a Full Gospel Businessmen's chapter meeting that was being broadcast live on the radio. He brought me up on stage to share what God had done for me. Although my dad was plugged in to the Holy Spirit, he didn't have a lot of social skills. However, he did the best he could with what he had.

I had seen God do many miracles for people when my dad prayed. I loved seeing God work through my dad like that. He supported me at the Full Gospel meetings and at church. Unfortunately, he didn't really know how to help me at home or in the other areas of my life. He didn't really know how to help me become a disciple, that is, a mature follower of Christ who thought, spoke, and acted, just like Jesus. But God knew what I needed to learn.

I remember God teaching me truth from the Bible that started correcting the lies I had believed...

Even as a teenager, I remember God teaching me truth from the Bible that began correcting the lies I had believed. I was so full of wrong thoughts and beliefs. I was sure everyone would make fun of me. I learned later in life these are called "Cognitive distortions." I call them "stinking thinking." Getting rid of "stinking thinking" is a process. But you have to start somewhere and sometime to deal with it if you are going to get rid of it.

I began studying the Bible and spending all my spare time praying and worshiping the Lord. Many teenagers hang out with their friends. Because I had never learned to make friends, there wasn't anyone to hang out with except the Lord.

When I told my parents God wanted me to go to Bible College, my dad left the room and started crying because he thought I had finally developed brain damage. He did not believe I could ever take care of myself, much less go to college or be a minister of the gospel. When I was a senior in High School, we went to the International Bible College in San Antonio, Texas for a visit. My parents just knew that the College would not accept me because I couldn't take care of myself physically. I couldn't feed myself; I needed help getting dressed; I couldn't button my shirt.

During the interview process, we met David Coote, the president of the college. He was getting ready to tell my parents that the college was not set up to accommodate the physically-challenged. As he turned around to tell them that, what came out of his mouth was, "Chuck's going to make us a wonderful student."

A long time afterwards, he told me, "I did not plan to say that!"

God was so good to give my dad a front row seat to a miracle in my life when the president of the college accepted me as a student!

I received a partial scholarship to college but I also had to work during college to pay for the rest. I had no concept of the costs involved or how I would be able to work and go to school at the same time. During a chapel meeting in my senior year, the president of the college called me up in front of the assembly. He told the students about me and the major physical challenges I had. Then he told the students that I was graduating with no debt! I had worked during the summers and also during the school year to pay my way through.

"If Chuck can do that with his challenges, what's your excuse?" he said. It was a little embarrassing for the College

President to say that about me. On the other hand, I recognized that it was God's favor on my life that made it possible to graduate debt-free. I still pray for God to give me favor every day and you can, too.

I also experienced much favor at my job in my senior year of college. The building contractor I worked for encouraged me to bring two other guys from the college to do the work I was doing. His business was booming and I had to put in too many hours to keep up. My new job was to supervise their work.

I asked the supervisor why he needed two people. He said, "Because it will take two people to do the work you have been doing!"

Although I had physical challenges, God had given me a good work ethic. I got my team started at 1pm and checked back on their work at 5 to make sure they'd done what they were supposed to do. I got paid a full salary as a supervisor and also helped my friends get the jobs they needed so they could pay for school. I used that time every afternoon to work on my senior thesis and got paid in the process. God is so creative! He not only took care of my needs financially, He also took care of my friend's financial needs.

But let me back up for a moment. During my first year of college, I became friends with a couple of young ladies. They met me every time we ate at the dining hall and helped me get the food onto my plate and into my mouth. We all ate at the dining hall at long tables. The food was passed from one person to the next just as you would pass the food around the table at home. Well, although that sounds real simple, I couldn't do it.

The involuntary movements of my upper body made it impossible. My hands and arms had a mind of their own at times! I could very well end up throwing the food at the next person at the table instead of passing it gently because I couldn't control my movements. I really didn't want to start an accidental food fight.

So I prayed, "Lord, you're going to have to send somebody to help me, or I'm going to be on a long fast. Lord, I don't really want to go on a four-year fast!"

These ladies felt impressed by the Holy Spirit to help me at every meal. They would sit right next to me during meals. One would put food on my plate while the other fed me. I am so thankful for those ladies. I was afraid for a while that I was going to lose a lot of weight in college.

The first year, they helped me eat every day and my roommate helped me button my shirt. The second year, they didn't have to feed me anymore. Then in the third year, I didn't need any help at all with buttoning my shirt or eating. I got progressively better each year. You know, sometimes we see an instant miracle and complete healing. There are also gradual healings where we get better a little bit at a time. Mine has been gradual, and it's almost finished! Hallelujah!

I met a family in Bible College who were remarkable. This family was willing to mentor and teach me the life skills I did not get growing up. And now, through my counseling ministry, God is teaching other people the life skills they need to learn to live healthy lives.

The husband of the family mentored me in college. We talked through a lot of issues. When I was with his family, they included me in everything they did as a family. Many of the life skills I learned came from that time in my life when he mentored me. The parents interacted so well with each other and with their children. I wanted to learn about how a healthy family operated from them. I watched how the husband and wife conducted their family, how they treated each other and the kids. Most of the time I was with them, my mouth was hanging open in amazement.

"Oh, so that's how it works. That's how a healthy family should interact," I said to myself over and over.

My family was dysfunctional in a number of ways. It was amazing for me to see this family that functioned so well with each other.

One time, the dad called the two kids in to the living room and said, "Your mom and I are about to have a conflict and we wanted you to see how we work through it."

We all sat down, including me, and we observed a husband and wife working through a real issue with honor and respect. I saw how a conflict could be worked through with honesty, humility, vulnerability, and intimacy for the first time. Wow, I was so impressed! That family changed my life. I started to develop hope for my future family as I saw how they lived.

God wanted me to be set free, but He also wanted me to help other people get free as they learned the life skills I had learned.

As I write this book, I am mentoring another young man. My prayer is that he will learn as much from me as I learned from my mentors years ago. I met this young man at church. After we talked for a while, I told him how great it was to meet him and talk with him. Then I gave him a hug. After that hug, he told me, "When you hugged me, it felt like I was being hugged by my father for the first time."

I realized that the Holy Spirit was ministering to him. So, we set up our first meeting. I love it when God puts things together. Over the years, I've mentored a number of people through my counseling ministry. I also mentored many other people as we hung out and did things together. Mentoring someone is different from delivering a 3-point sermon. It's a process of interacting honestly and lovingly with someone else so they can learn what you know.

Is there anyone in your life whom you could mentor? If you ask the Holy Spirit, He may bring someone to mind. You may be in a place where you need to be mentored. The same Holy Spirit can bring someone to mind who you could ask to help mentor you. The Holy Spirit is our teacher. Actually, Jesus is the best mentor I've ever had. It is so exciting that God lets us be part of the mentoring process with each other.

The objective of mentoring is that we become mature.

One of the main objectives of mentoring is that we become mature. Another way we talk about being mature is to use the word discipleship. A disciple learns what the teacher presents. His life is changed as he does what the teacher says to do. After a while, the disciple should look very similar to the teacher in terms of how he solves problems, interacts with others, and prioritizes his life.

As you read this book, my prayer is that the principles I'm teaching you will change your life. I hope that some of the stories and truths you learn from this book will stay with you for the rest of your life.

I don't want to burst your bubble, but all of us have something about us that's not perfect. Some of us are less perfect than others but all of us qualify as sinners who have problems.

Romans 5:8 says, *"But God showed his great love for us by sending Christ to die for us while we were still sinners."* For us to be less than perfect just qualifies us to be saved and healed by God. You have to know you need help and have problems in order to be saved. Of course, we always want it to be somebody else who has a problem, don't we? It's always easier to see the problems other people go through than it is to look at our own issues.

I am so thankful for what God has done in my life. *The problems I had were opportunities for God to do miracles in my life*. God doesn't send us sickness and harm. He is a good Father. Good fathers don't do that kind of thing to their kids. However God *does* work out all the problems and issues and circumstances in our lives for our good because He loves us.

Romans 8:28 says, *"And we know that God causes everything to work together for the good of those who love God and are called according to his purpose for them."*

Another job I had while in Bible College was working at a chemical plant. There was a particular chemical they used at the plant to clean out the inside of drains. This chemical would eat anything in its path, and it was so incredible! Just for fun, we would put things in the big vat where this chemical was made and watch them dissolve. I remember taking a stick with a rag on the end of it and dipping it into the vat just to see the whole thing disintegrate. It dissolved anything.

So, we workers were always told, "You've got to wear protective eyewear, rubber aprons, and rubber gloves when you're working with that chemical." That made sense. I sure didn't want to look like that rag I dissolved.

One day, I was in the warehouse stocking some of the various chemical products in boxes to take them out to the showroom. A salesman had been showing a customer this drain cleaning chemical and didn't put it away correctly. He put the bottle up on top of one of the stacks of boxes and forgot to screw the lid on tight. I came with another stack of boxes on the dolly and set the load right next to the stack that had the open bottle on it. It kind of jiggled the stack and the open bottle of chemicals came right down on top of me. Right there, I had my first chemical shower and it was not good! Sirens were going off and they hosed me down with water. My eye went black; I couldn't see a thing out of my right eye. I could feel the chemical immediately starting to eat my skin.

The people helping me began to scream, "Oh, no! Oh, no! He looks terrible!"

I'm thinking, "That's just great. If it wasn't my body, it might be cool to see this. I bet it looks really gross!" But this was my body they were talking about!

Someone called 911. All my skin was beginning to disintegrate and melt. As I was on my way to the hospital in the ambulance, one of the other students who worked at the chemical plant called the Bible College and asked them to pray. The whole student body of the college started praying right away. Those kids knew how to pray! **I am so glad I went to a powerful Bible College where the students and the teachers believed in the supernatural power of God to heal.**

They wrapped me in bandages at the plant. As they took me to the hospital in the ambulance, they talked with the doctor in the emergency room.

I heard the paramedic say, "I don't think there's any hope for the eye; I think the eye's completely gone."

All I could feel was burning on my skin. When I got to the emergency room, they unwrapped the bandages around my face. The doctor looked at me. All of a sudden he said, "Why did you bring him here? I mean, there's a couple little red marks on his cheek, but there's nothing seriously wrong."

The eye was completely normal, no scar tissue... nothing. I was completely healed by the power of God. Wow!

There is nothing too hard for God!

Friend, there's nothing that's too hard for our God...**nothing**. In Numbers Chapter 11, there is a great story. Moses was talking to God and said, "You know God, the children of Israel are tired of eating manna. They want to eat meat, and where are You going to get enough meat to feed all these people?"

Then Moses began telling God all the reasons it couldn't be done. "If you took every animal that exists and every fowl of the air, there wouldn't be enough meat to feed all these people," Moses said. I love God's response in verse 23. "When did I become weak? Now you shall see whether my word comes true or not!" (TLB)

Isn't that great! There's nothing too hard for God. No matter what kind of problem you have in your life, God is here to help you. It doesn't matter if it's a physical issue or an emotional one: God is not weak, His power has not diminished.

Hebrews 13:8 says, *"Jesus Christ is the same yesterday, and today, and forever."*   Here is the best news ever: God wants to help you.

John 10:10 says, *"The thief's purpose is to steal and kill and destroy. My purpose is to give them a rich and satisfying life."*

In **2 Corinthians 5:17**, Paul says, *"This means that anyone who belongs to Christ has become a new person. The old life is gone; a new life has begun!"*

Prayer...

Father God, thank You for being the same yesterday, today,

and forever. I give You my heart and ask You to make me new.

There is nothing too hard for You. Thank You, Father, that Your

purpose for me is to live a rich and satisfying life. Thank You

for being faithful to complete the good work You have started

in my life. Thank you that my old life is gone and my new life in

You has begun! In the name of Jesus Christ, Amen.

Chapter 4 - Car Accident

I slowly woke up in the hospital bed. The first thing I noticed was the light. It was a regular fluorescent light like you would see anywhere.

"I must not be dead," I thought. "Heaven would have a better lighting system than this."

Then I saw the IVs attached to my arm and some other wires that went from my body to the machines monitoring my vital signs. I wasn't sure what had happened. The last thing I remembered, I was on my way home from a Bible Study with a married couple who were friends of mine. They were in the front seat, I was in the back. I was sitting on the edge of the back seat with my head stretched up as far as I could so I could talk with them. We were on I-25 in Denver and there was an accident up ahead. Traffic was at a standstill and we were at the back of the line. That was all I remembered.

As the days went by, I found out the rest of the story. Our car was hit from behind by a drunk driver who apparently didn't see the traffic jam. He was still going sixty miles per hour when he hit us. The police said that if I had been sitting back in the seat like you're supposed to sit, I would have been dead. The back seat was completely destroyed. I would have been destroyed also had I been sitting back. Even though I was sitting forward in the seat, the impact of the crash pushed the back seat on top of me so I was trapped. I guess it's okay to break the rules at times! I wasn't trying to be rebellious by not wearing my seat belt and sitting so far up in the car. I was just so excited to talk with my friends about what God was doing.

Things had been going so well in my life up until this point. I had a great job as a supervisor for my friend's construction company where I managed a large crew of guys. I did this during the summers while I was attending Bible College. After I finished Bible College, I got married. Before long, we had a beautiful daughter. I preached at revival meetings and saw people getting saved all the time. I thought everything was working well.

I thought things were going so well and then my world turned upside down when we were hit by that car.

The years between college and the car accident were miraculous for me. After a lifetime of feeling invisible people actually listened to what I said in the workplace and did what I told them to do. Thousands paid attention when I spoke at evangelistic meetings. I never dreamed people would listen to me or respect me like this when I was a kid. I thought things were going so well and then my world turned upside down when we were hit by that car.

The doctor said I would never be the same again. He told me that the injuries I had would be with me my entire life. My marriage was already in trouble. This accident was the straw that broke the camel's back. My (first) marriage did not survive this accident. I was in traction so I couldn't do anything to stop all the losses that were happening. I lost my job, of course. I couldn't supervise the guys on the job site from my hospital bed, so I had to be replaced. I became depressed, angry, and critical. One time, a nurse came in and asked how I was doing.

I heard myself snap at her, "How do you think I'm doing? I'm in pain because I just lost my health, my job, and my family!"

That night when I was alone, I saw how angry and sarcastic I really was. I cried out to God, "What do You want me to do?"

"I want you to give what you need."

Just after I prayed, I heard the voice of God. It wasn't an audible voice, but it was a clear, distinct voice that rose up from deep inside me. "Encourage hurting people," was what I heard God say.

"But God, don't I qualify?" I figured I was hurting just as much as anyone else in there.

He said, "I want you to give what you need."

I didn't get it at first. I wanted to be encouraged so badly and now God is telling me to encourage other people? It wasn't until later I realized I had to give away what I so desperately needed so God was free to encourage me and to heal me. We reap what we sow. If you need to be encouraged, look for someone to encourage. If you need God to heal you, look for someone else you can pray for who also needs healing. That revelation was a living word from God to me. It was a turning point in my ministry.

Sowing before we reap is a principle of God's Kingdom. If I need encouragement, God says I need to sow encouragement by encouraging other people. If I need physical healing, I need to do what I can to help other people walk in the healing that they need. Many people we see who get well in our ministry have to renew their minds. It is God's job to heal. However, God says we are to get involved in the process of renewing our minds.

Romans 12:2 says, *"Don't copy the behavior and customs of this world, but let God transform you into a new person by changing the way you think. Then you will learn to know God's will for you, which is good and pleasing and perfect."*

God cannot bless what He has cursed and He cannot curse what He has blessed (Numbers 22:6b). Up until this point during my hospital stay, I felt sorry for myself. I went back and forth between anger and depression about my situation. I didn't realize that those things were not pleasing to God. I had myself at the center of my world. That is not the way God wants us to live. To be blunt, selfishness is sin. God has cursed sin.

Therefore, He will never bless the things we do that come out of our sinful nature.

As I began to look for people I could pray for and encourage, I saw the blessing of the Lord rest on me. God will always bless us when we walk in obedience to Him. He will always bless us when we agree with Him and start to obey what He asks us to do.

How do we deal with voices in our heads encouraging us to believe the wrong things? How do we resist those voices and do the right things even when we don't feel like it? How did Jesus deal with temptation? What did He do to walk in victory all the time? In Matthew Chapters 3 and 4, you can read the story.

1. Before He started His ministry, He went to the Jordan River and was baptized. By that act, Jesus indicated He would follow and obey God with His whole heart. That's what baptism means in the New Testament.

2. He was filled with the Holy Spirit while still in the Jordan River. Then the Holy Spirit led Him into the desert for forty days where He fasted and prayed.

3. When satan came to tempt Him, He answered back with scripture that the Holy Spirit brought to His mind. He used the strength of the Holy Spirit, not His own strength. When you have been fasting for forty days, you have no strength left in yourself.

We have to follow the same plan Jesus did.

1. Make a decision to follow Jesus and obey Him.

2. Ask the Holy Spirit to fill you. Jesus said if we ask the Father to give us the Holy Spirit, He will.

3. **When you are tempted, rely on the Holy Spirit. Use the Bible, just as Jesus did.** Use the power of the Holy Spirit, just like Jesus did. Stand on the truth, resist the devil, and keep on standing. That's what Jesus did and that's what we can do also.

As a believer, I could help people in the hospital see how much God loved them. There are many Christians who don't act like believers or share their faith with other people. They seem to be afraid to share about Jesus. As a result, they don't practice doing the things God says to do. When God told me to encourage hurting people, I decided to become a practicing believer instead of someone who hid his faith. I could help others work through their pain, discouragement, and anger. I could help them find hope again.

Hope is necessary for faith to activate. I was in a room with three beds and there were many people coming in and out. Some stayed for a day, some for a week or more. I prayed for everyone who let me. Actually, I even prayed for the people who didn't want me to pray for them. I just didn't tell them I was praying.

One of the things I did was play cassette tapes of the Bible all the time. Even when I went to sleep, I had a tape going. It not only kept me focused on God, it also opened the door for me to talk about the Bible and God with whomever came into the room. I'm sure some of them thought I was a nut. I decided I was going to be a little bit crazy for God no matter what anyone else thought. A lot of people got saved because they came into my room and heard the Bible playing. It was easy for me to start a conversation with them about God. I found out that if I talked to everyone I met about Jesus, some of them would ask Him to come into their hearts just like I did when I was sixteen.

When I first started encouraging other people, I wasn't feeling it at all. I didn't have enough faith to blow the fuzz off a peanut. The words of encouragement I was sharing were the words I needed to hear. As I focused my heart and attention on helping other people, God encouraged me. At times I wanted to take notes about what the Holy Spirit was leading me to share with people so I could go over it again later. As I saw God perform miracles in other people I prayed for, my body started to get well. My faith increased for my own healing as I saw God heal others through my prayers.

God did not cause that drunk driver to hit us that day. Neither did He make a decision that I should be in traction. Good fathers don't harm their children like that! The man who hit us made the decision to drink and drive. **What God did was turn that awful situation around for His glory.**

My dad and I told my testimony at a Full Gospel Businessmen's meeting about how God healed me. It got back to the Chaplain at Craig Hospital. He asked my dad and me to speak at a Chapel service. Before long, I was going there every month to minister. Not much longer after that, they asked me to be a volunteer Chaplain at Craig Hospital to provide pastoral care for the patients. (I used to drive past Craig Hospital every day before the accident without giving the patients in there a second thought. After my accident, I had a new desire to pray and minister to people at the hospital.) I've been a volunteer Chaplain at Craig Hospital for almost 40 years. We have seen so many people miraculously healed by God's power. We have prayed with hundreds of people to accept Jesus. We have also seen many families restored by God's grace

Now, I knew how hard it was to be a patient in the hospital. I also knew how lonely it was to have your life pulled out from under you. The doctors and nurses do such a great job at the hospital. But, they can only do so much.

One day, during the time I was still injured and at Colorado General Hospital, I was able to encourage a hospital administrator. While we were talking she broke down and cried. She was an administrator in charge of the Physical Therapy Department. She consulted with my therapist about specific patients. During one of our conversations, I led her to the Lord. There were a number of doctors and nurses who received the Lord because God gave me the opportunity to share with them.

She appreciated my encouragement so much that as soon as I was able to, she allowed me go to all the floors in the hospital and encourage everyone I wanted to. The favor of God was on me as I went all over the hospital and encouraged everyone who listened.

Philippians 1:6 says, *"And I am certain that God, who began the good work within you, will continue his work until it is finally finished on the day when Christ Jesus returns."*

One of the people I prayed for at Aurora Regional Hospital was a roofer. Someone at work had gotten mad at him and pushed him off a roof. He was paralyzed from the neck down. The situation was even more tragic when I learned he had two young children at home. I knew God wanted him to be healed so he could play with his kids and be the father and husband he needed to be in his family. I prayed for him every day for a couple of months. He got better and better until he walked out of the hospital. Later, I found out that two other believers were praying for him every night for those same two months. I was praying during the day and they were praying at night.

Greg and Ralph prayed for the patients at Aurora Regional Hospital 5-6 nights a week for 3 months straight. When we prayed for the roofer, we didn't know God had us on the same assignment to pray for the sick and didn't meet until after he was healed. Over the years, Greg and I got to know each other quite well.

I love **Romans 8:38**. *"And I am convinced that nothing can ever separate us from God's love. Neither death nor life, neither angels nor demons, neither our fears for today nor our worries about tomorrow—not even the powers of hell can separate us from God's love."*

I don't know what pain, what injury, or what disease you are living with. But I do know that God loves you and is eager to help you in every area of your life. He is not too busy. There is not anyone in the world more important to God than you. He cares about you enough to number every hair on your head. One of the best prayers I know is really simple and easy to remember: "Help!" Like a flood, the Holy Spirit is ready to help you. Are you ready to ask Him for help?

Are you ready to ask Him for help?

During this season of my life, I was learning to counsel people. I held evangelistic meetings in Canada before my car accident and even more after God healed me of those injuries. Before the evening meetings, people would ask if they could talk to me about their problems. The Holy Spirit would give me words to tell them. Many of them got delivered. I knew that people could be delivered from problems through prayer; however, God was teaching me that people can also be delivered from problems through counseling.

I took counseling classes in college but thought my main gifting was evangelism. Over the years, I found out that almost everyone needs counseling at some level, even after they accept Jesus. When the Holy Spirit gives us truth and we speak that truth to someone in love, transformation can occur. When we learn to speak the truth to each other in love, we can help each other grow up into the fullness of Christ.

Prayer...

Lord Jesus, teach me to love other people the way You love me. Give me the grace to receive Your love for me. In the name of Jesus Christ, Amen.

Chapter 5 - Chaplain and Counselor

I was in the building of a large corporation in downtown Denver, talking to one of the CEOs. His office was completely surrounded by windows and I was very taken with the view.

I asked him, "How do you get any work done with a view like this from your office?"

"I know. Sometimes it's hard," he said. "I have to be very intentional about focusing on my work at times."

We talked for an hour and a half about miracles and the reality of Jesus Christ. I love to talk about that! He was amazed as I told him the things God had done in my life. I told him about the presence of Jesus Christ and how eager He is to heal. As I shared stories with him about people that God healed, it became clear to him that God loves every one of us and wants to do exceedingly abundantly above all that we can ask or think. I prayed with him about the specific issues he had. He told me later, that God answered our prayers.

As a society, we have not done a good job of helping each other work through disagreements and conflicts. It has become acceptable for kids in school to act out if you offend them. That dynamic is true for many adults too

I worked for a police agency for a few years as a Victim's Advocate and Chaplain. I worked with several other police agencies in the State of Colorado. One night during a ride-along with an officer, he told me "Now I don't want you to run that

Jesus stuff down my throat. I don't believe in God and I don't want to talk about anything related to God or religion. Are we clear?"

I told him, "No problem, you're the one wearing the gun. I believe Jesus is just too good to cram down anyone's throat. I won't say a word."

From 7 pm until 9 pm, we talked about football and other odds and ends. He shared some of the "dumb criminal" stories he had experienced. One of the calls he told me about was a burglary. The guy who broke into the house ran out the back door into the open field when he heard the police arrive. It was dark and he figured no one would be able to see him. He was surprised when the police walked right up to where he was hiding even though he made all sorts of zigzag moves in the field.

He asked them, "How did you find me?"

The officer told him, "You probably shouldn't have worn those shoes tonight." His shoes had lights on them that flashed when he ran.

It took a couple hours of riding with the officer before he opened up and started telling me about his problems. I just listened. He was testing me to see if I would respect his boundary and not talk about God. When he started talking about his teenagers, I thought, "Now, that's getting a little closer to home."

Then he said, "Sometimes I just wonder where God is."

"You're the one who brought Him up," I said. We laughed.

He told me that the reason he brought God up was because I did what I said I would do. I didn't break the boundary he had set. He trusted me because I kept my word. I would have lost the chance to talk with him about God if I had tried to bring God into the conversation before he did.

I was also a victim's advocate for the police department. I went on a call one night. A lady had been beaten up by her boyfriend. They were strapping her onto the stretcher to take her to the ambulance. Lying on the gurney, she just stared straight up in the air.

You are way too valuable to be treated this way!

I stepped up to her and said, "Ma'am, I am so sorry that this happened to you tonight. The truth is, you are way too valuable to be treated this way."

She looked at me and said, "What did you say?"

"Well, I just said that I'm sorry that this happened to you and you're way too valuable to be treated this way."

She had me repeat it three times to her. She then said, "You know, you're the only man that's ever told me that I'm way too valuable to be treated like this."

I said, "That saddens me that I'm the only man that's ever told you that but I'm excited at the same time to be the first real man to tell you the truth. You are way too valuable to be treated this way."

That night, a paradigm shift happened in her life. She got it. She had a total breakthrough. She said, "I'm way too valuable to be treated this way."

By the time she got to the ambulance, we heard her yelling that phrase at the top of her lungs. It was so exciting! I loved it. I told the officers while we were still in the living room of her home, "I don't think she will be back, she got it".

Often, people who are involved in abusive relationships end up going back to live with that abusive partner because that's how they think relationships work. She shifted away from her maladaptive belief that she was not valuable and received a true revelation of who she was. She was affirming it and declaring it at the top of her lungs.

Jesus said in **John 8:36**, *"So if the Son sets you free, you are truly free."*

It is so exciting to see people set free from cognitive distortions. A cognitive distortion, as shared earlier, is a thought that causes individuals to perceive reality inaccurately. I call it "Stinking Thinking." In a nut shell, "Stinking Thinking" is when you believe lies about who you are and how the world works. When we live on the basis of those lies, we get into many kinds of bondage and trouble. **When those lies are broken, we are free to move forward into the truth**. The best way to break the lies is to hear and receive the truth.

If you are a victim in an abusive relationship, you need to call 1-800-799-7233 right now and talk to someone because, "You are way too valuable to be treated that way." You can call this number for free advice and help if you are in an abusive relationship. If this phone number doesn't work, look up The National Domestic Violence Hotline number and make your call.

Another time I was called in to talk with a lady who was held up at gun point. She was in shock and the police officers couldn't get her to say anything about what had happened or about her attackers. When I came up, I told her that I couldn't even imagine having a shotgun right up in my face. She told me that she could see the trigger finger shaking on the guy who held the gun. She said her life flashed before her eyes.

I told her, "Well, at least you know you're not co-dependent. If you were co-dependent, then someone else's life would have flashed before your eyes."

She laughed. I was able to talk with her and get two pages of information about what happened and the guys who were involved with the robbery. When I gave the information to the police they were shocked and wanted to know how I got her to talk. That night, I taught them some of the skills for life that are in this book. When I empathized with her and got her to respond to some humor, she opened up. Her shock was reduced by the humor. As I listened using the Speaker-Listener technique, she felt safe to share things with me because she realized I was really listening. (The Speaker-Listener technique is mentioned in the back of the book under Life Skills)

Empathy is a powerful tool in the workplace and also at home. When a husband is not empathetic with his wife, it's like they are both in a pool and she's in the deep end. The water is over her head and she can't swim. When you are not empathetic, it's like saying, "Why are you drowning? Come on, swim over to the edge! What a silly thing for you to do...drown in a pool when the edge is just 15 feet away. You are such a loser."

When you interact with empathy, it's like going out to help a drowning person get out of the water. Wrap a thick warm towel around their shoulders, and let their breathing come back to normal. When you do that, you are setting everything else aside to make sure they are safe. After a person is safe and calmed down, you use the same focus to try and find out where they are coming from. It's not really the time to figure out who's right and who may be wrong. It's not the time to focus on emotional or extreme behavior.

As men, we tend to focus on the appearance of how another person is acting instead of looking hard at what circumstances may be causing them to act that way. Empathy is focusing on understanding the other person, not making sure the other person understands us.

Humor is another powerful tool we can use to help other people. It's also a powerful tool we can use to help ourselves. I still had quite a few problems with the upper part of my body. I still had many involuntary movements from the Cerebral Palsy I developed at birth.

While I was speaking on the Trinity Broadcasting Network (TBN), I shared about a time when someone came up to me and said, "So what's wrong with you?"

I said, "Well, there are a lot of things wrong with me. Where do you want me to start?"

He said, "What's wrong with your head? How come you keep shaking like that?"

I said, "Oh, man, that's nothing. Sometimes it spins clear around."

After the interview, one of the camera guys came up to me and said, "I'd like to see that."

"OK," I told him, "Watch real close."

I spun my whole body around.

"Do you want to see it again?"

Sometimes it helps to look at things with a bit of humor, especially your personal challenges. I will certainly not let some of the involuntary movements my body still does at times keep me from walking in the anointing and favor of God. Many people have a long list of reasons for not doing the things God wants them to do. We come up with all kinds of considerations that become excuses for not walking the way God says we should walk. It's important to step out and obey God before you have everything figured out. Before you have everything perfect in your life, it's important to take the very next step of faith.

Paul said in **2 Corinthians 12:9**, *"My grace is all you need. My power works best in weakness."*

One of the couples I counseled shared this story.

"It was remarkable to see you interact with us. In one session, my wife was upset about something and you asked her to tell you about it. You stayed engaged with her as she went through ten minutes or so of venting. I saw you paying attention, asking her how she felt when those things happened and I saw you empathize with her and how she was feeling. You were focused on standing in her shoes and understanding how she felt. After just a few minutes, the event was over and she could talk about what was going on without the meltdown behavior or even her strong emotions taking over the room. It seemed like you humbled yourself low enough to go right under her defenses and after a few minutes the whole thing was over and you could talk with her easily and plainly. You went low enough to slip under her wall of anger. By listening and asking sincere questions, you went under the defensive wall she had built.

When the dust cleared, you were standing with her inside the walls she had built. From there, it was easy for both of you to knock the walls of anger down and talk about the real problem that triggered the anger."

"That meeting changed my life. I have changed how I talk with my wife as a result. When I hear her frustration level rise or when we start to misunderstand each other, I go low. I focus on trying to understand and I stop trying to be understood. I start to do what I saw you do in our counseling session and when I do that, I get the same result you got. For years, I thought conflict resolution was about one of us being right and the other person wrong. Through your example, I am learning that both of us will need to have help at times to get through a problem. I need to make sure I focus on understanding what my wife is going through so we can work on solving the problems we face together."

The purpose of the life skills is to get this kind of result. I'm so glad the couple shared this with me. I'm also glad they learned to use a tool that helped them resolve a problem. Having tools is important, but you still have to work with those tools and develop skills using them before they will work the way they should.

Honor and respect are like the foundation of a house.

I learned a lot about honor and respect from the Olsen family when I was in college. Honor and respect are like the foundation of a house. When they are correctly set in place, all the other life skills can be incorporated together and built on that firm foundation.

The Olsen's were a family at my home church. They ministered to young people, like myself, by including us in their life. They took us on vacations and mission trips with them and mentored us.

I had to see the Olsen's model honor and respect for me in their home before I could get a handle on it. I didn't even know how to receive a compliment. I had to see all those interpersonal exchanges occur before my eyes before I could understand how they worked.

In many counseling sessions, I've asked the client, "Did you hear what they just said?"

"No" is a very normal response.

"What did you hear them say?"

When they know they will have to mirror back what the other person said, they tend to listen a lot closer. It's embarrassing to get what someone is saying wrong over and over. I know that for a fact because I did it. If they didn't mirror it back correctly, the person sharing would repeat it.

Often, we communicate a mixed message when we talk to another person. The reason some people don't want to listen to a compliment is that the compliment is subtly attached to a negative statement.

"Thanks for making the cabinet. Is that door straight? Maybe next time you could make it straighter."

Many people are not finishing with chores in the house because whatever they do will not be good enough. They procrastinate on the project and take the heat for not finishing because they feel that it's better than doing their best and finishing the project but not having it done well enough. If the task is not completed, they will never have to hear, "It's not good enough."

I still do a lot of chaplain work at Craig Hospital. However, my primary ministry is as a counselor and evangelist. I love to share my testimony in churches and invite the people there to meet the Jesus that I love so much. God has opened so many doors for me. I know He wants to open doors for you, also. Each of us has specific good deeds that God has prepared for us to do (**Ephesians 2:10**). All we need to do is listen carefully to Him and do what He says to do.

At a meeting, I was talking about boundaries. I could see a certain gentleman was getting agitated. He was giving me angry looks and squirming in his chair as I talked. I knew he was becoming upset with me for some reason. At the same time, I could also see that the rest of the people in the meeting were getting something out of my message.

At the end of the session, he came up to me and said, "I want to give you a piece of my mind".

Well, I knew I didn't want to hear what he had to say.

I said, "You're going to need every piece you've got," and walked away. I knew that what he was going to say was not going to be constructive. He was going to contaminate me and I didn't need that. Neither do you. That may sound like a harsh way to talk to someone, but sometimes, the most loving thing you can do is to speak clearly and directly to the people who confront you.

Words are so important and powerful. One person I talked to told me he wouldn't amount to anything his entire life. He dropped out of college with only one hour left to finish his degree. As we began processing some issues together, he realized that when his father told him he wouldn't amount to anything, he believed it so deeply that he dropped out of school before he finished. In his mind, if he had finished the degree it would have disproved what his dad told him. That negative word his father said, probably in anger, cut his soul and from that point on he began living as though what his father said was really true.

Over the years, he had minimized the impact of his dad's words over him and believed there were other reasons for his lack of success. He finally realized how powerful his dad's words actually had been. We identified the cognitive distortion and started replacing it with truth. That empowered him to overcome his false belief and go back to school to finish his degree. He began to see how important he was in God's eyes. He saw that he deserved to have everything God wanted him to have.   That degree was the first of many successful things he accomplished.

Often, it is just one thing that keeps you from walking in freedom and power.

There is nothing too hard for God. Anything that is holding us back can be defeated in the Name of Jesus Christ.

"For I can do everything through Christ, who gives me strength." It is a matter of combining His power with our ability and we go forward, hand in hand. God uses our ability and we use His power. He needs us and we need Him.

I remember a man I was counseling. We were going over a page about boundaries and he said, "This has got to be one of the most stupid things I have ever heard in my life."

I replied, "That doesn't sound like it is going to work for you".

He said, "No kidding."

"Well, listen," I said. "Here's my card; you're not teachable right now. When you are give me a call and we'll go to work."

He said, "You're not going to teach me?"

"No, you're not teachable now but you will be at some point. So, when you are, give me a call," I answered.

In a conflict situation, it's important to determine if the other person is teachable. If they are locked into their own opinion and agenda, you may as well save your breath.

He got so angry at what I said. Fifteen years later, he called me and he said, "I'm teachable now. Can we go to work?"

I said, "Absolutely."

As we picked up where we had left off in the sessions, he told me he kept my card on his dresser the whole time. He moved it to dust the top of his dresser and put my card right back. He said the reason he kept my card was that he knew I had told him the truth even though it had made him so mad.

"I wasn't ready. I wasn't teachable and you're the only one who had the guts to tell me the truth," he said.

As we began working together, he told me that when I confronted him in my office all those years ago about not being teachable, he was ready to punch me in the face. He made great progress in our sessions because now he was ready to learn.

Good news! God has a great plan for your life.

Have you ever felt that you don't know what God wants you to do specifically? I have good news for you; God has a great plan for your life. The truth is, He's called every one of us for a purpose and He can turn everything that's happened in your life around for good.

Romans 8:28 says, *"And we know that God causes everything to work together for the good of those who love Him and are called according to His purpose for them."*

The Bible also says in **Psalms 37:4**, " *Take delight in the LORD, and he will give you your heart's desires."*

A had a man come to me one day and say, "I really want to find out what the will of God is for me. I've never been able to find it."

I told him, "The will of God is really not that hard to find".

"Are you kidding me?" he said. "I've been trying to find it for years and haven't been able to. How do you do it?"

"Well, what's the desire of your heart?" I asked.

He said, "What's that got to do with the will of God?"

I said, "A lot. Just humor me for a minute and tell me what the desire of your heart is."

He thought for a minute and said, "Well, I want to race cars. See, that doesn't have anything to do with the will of God now, does it?"

I told him, "It has everything to do with the will of God. Do you know how many people there are on the race tracks that don't know Jesus? They won't listen to somebody like me, but they'll listen to you."

He was ecstatic! I thought he was going to kiss me! Today he's racing cars and having Bible studies in the pits. He has led many people to Jesus and is doing what he loves to do.

Prayer...

Thank You, Father, that You work everything together for good and that You give us the desires of our hearts as we follow You. Thank You for orchestrating every chapter of my life and loving me each step of the way. In the name of Jesus Christ, Amen.

Chapter 6 - Business Consultant

I remember talking with someone in my family who said, "You don't deserve to have that nice new car."

He told me on another occasion, "You sure don't deserve to have such a pretty wife."

He didn't like me very much. I actually believe he was jealous of me! Many people say critical things. I've learned to take the high road in conflict situations. The Holy Spirit has taught me to respond to statements like that by saying, "You are right, I certainly don't deserve it! Isn't God great? He gives us so many things we don't deserve."

I had a choice to make: I could have answered him unkindly or I could have done what I did and find a way to lighten the situation and bless God in the process. I had another choice: to become bitter or to get better. All of us have parts of our lives that are broken. We all need to learn to overcome difficulty and exercise a bit of "Holy Amnesia."

I think that's what Paul was referring to in **Philippians 3:13b-14** when he said, *"Forgetting the past and looking forward to what lies ahead, I press on to reach the end of the race and receive the heavenly prize for which God, through Christ Jesus, is calling us."*

The Bible says, *"as much as it depends on us, live at peace with one another"* (**Romans 12:18**). We are only responsible to handle our own part in a godly way. We cannot control other people. All of us have conflicts. Learning to work through these conflicts is part of growing up. In my life, it was the mentor I met in college who helped me learn to operate differently.

The mentoring dynamic works in business also. Many businesses operate in a dysfunctional way because the people who work there are dysfunctional. All companies have people to do the work and most people I know have had to learn life skills. I have seen dramatic changes in corporate settings when I have counseled employees. Workshops, group sessions, and individual sessions can be specifically targeted to help the people who operate in a dysfunctional way

One employee I worked with was referred by his supervisor because the employee was interacting with other people at work like sandpaper. He was abrasive and difficult to get along with.

The supervisor told me, "I don't want to fire him but he's given me every reason in the book to do so. He's such a valuable employee because he knows the job so well but we have to get over the bumps in the road."

First, I had a session with the employee. Then I sat down with the employee and the supervisor at the same time. They needed a third party to be involved to ensure they stayed on track. The supervisor told me later that the dynamic changed when a third party had been present in the room. The employee didn't use the derogatory and inflammatory language because I was there at the meeting.

"He didn't want to be embarrassed by saying toxic things when you were there."

I started meeting with the employee privately and in small group settings. We began to paint a picture of what goals he had for his job.

I asked him, "Do you want to have this job for a year or two and then move on?"

He replied, "No, I would love to make this business my career."

I told him I could teach him how to do that. "If you're willing to hear the hard things I have to teach you, you could eventually become the CEO of this company."

He lit up like a Christmas tree. I told him that the things he was saying would prevent him from becoming CEO. When someone keeps saying angry and disrespectful things to others, they are making it harder for themselves to get along with those same people. It is like digging a hole in the path and you continually fall into that same hole.

"You can keep on digging holes for yourself to climb out of by talking the way you have been, or you can begin to learn the things you need to know to become CEO. I can teach you how to talk so you will move up in this business."

His supervisor told me, "It's been like night and day for him!"

It does not take long to see very dramatic changes. Often, all it takes is for the individual to look at the situation from a new perspective.

In business settings, we are very comfortable paying for help to solve problems that will make the company more profitable. I worked with a number of people in that same company. At the five-year point, the same supervisor told me, "We have saved hundreds of thousands of dollars as a company because of your counseling sessions. We have had no turnover of employees and, as a result, no costs incurred to train new people." I give God the glory for that because I was simply teaching them the things that God had taught me.

As a society, we have not done a good job of learning how to work through conflicts. Most businesses would benefit by learning to use the Life Skills. I can say that with confidence because all the businesses I know about have people who work there and who need to learn life skills.

I also worked with various police agencies for approximately ten years. I have gone on many ride-along trips with officers who didn't want to use their personal time for a counseling session. Some of the officers wanted to talk with me and some of them didn't. I always started out listening. That seems pretty simple, but you'd be surprised how many people forget to do that. Then, I focused on teaching the basic tools and skills so they could work with their team and also deal with the challenging people they had to face each day. If you think your job is hard, try being a police officer for a few days.

As my private clients began seeing good results in their own lives, they started seeing things in their workplaces that were not productive. They recommended me to their supervisors and coworkers. As a result, God opened doors for me to hold seminars and workshops in the corporate setting, and positive changes began to happen in those businesses.

It is amazing how quickly hope can rise in a group of people when they see concrete positive results in a short period. A few of the companies were willing to pay the counseling fee and also pay the employee their hourly rate to come to the session. Not all businesses are set up to do this, but it certainly makes it easier for the employee who may need help. They may not have seen me to work through their issues if they had had to pay for it or do it on their own time. From the business owner's standpoint, a few sessions may get them back an employee who can help the business earn thousands of dollars. It is expensive to train new employees and it often takes time to find the people who are the right fit for their company.

My first anger management classes were initiated because one of the other counselors in our building didn't want to teach the classes anymore. I was actually praying for more clients and this was one of the ways God answered my prayers.

A man in one of those group sessions was big, strong, and intimidating. He was behaving badly in our group. It seemed as though he was doing everything he could to get kicked out. I had a sense that that was his purpose so I didn't do it. He disagreed with everything I said. When other people shared, he was disrespectful. He looked like a time bomb ready to go off. In one session he was escalating as he had done before. This time, however, I asked him a different question.

"Who hurt you?" I asked in a soft voice. It was very quiet, you could have heard a pin drop.

Angrily, he said, "A lot of people have hurt me!"

I said, "Who do you think of specifically when I ask you that question?"

Then he answered sarcastically, "My Dad!"

And I said, "Well, now do you see why you've had such a problem with authority figures?"

He answered me sarcastically again, "Not until right now!"

That was a paradigm shift in his life. From that day on, he was the best member in my class. When any of the other guys acted up, he would just look at them and they got the message.

We had a couple of new guys show up who were disrespectful to me during their first session. I was surprised when he said to them, "You should listen to him. He knows what he's talking about."

When they came for the second session, he sat right beside them and they became wonderful students also. I was a little bit sad when he finished his time with us in that class. I liked having him as an advocate.

In one of the sessions, we talked about road rage. One of the men shared that every day as he went to work, he was looking for someone to get mad at. Part of his routine was to pick out a poor driver and gravitate toward them so he could catch him doing something wrong. He said his mouth would start watering when he spotted someone and started heading over to drive close to them. He had a visceral response to the rage. He would get to express that anger very soon.

I don't know about you, but I'm not a perfect driver. I have been known to make a mistake or two over the years. I was surprised when some other guys in the group said they did the same thing. Anger is a normal response for us as people. It is important that we learn how to deal with it correctly. The Bible says that Jesus got angry and we know that He didn't sin. We need to learn how to operate the way Jesus did.

I have helped a number of church leaders work through conflicts with each other and with people in their church. Does that sound odd? It really shouldn't because pastors and church leaders are people too. That means they are not perfect. That is one thing all of us have in common; we are not perfect. The people who think they are, are the ones you have to watch out for! If you think you're perfect, you're living in denial.

Once while attending a Full Gospel Businessmen's Conference, halfway through the conference, I woke up with a sore eye. It was the most pain I had ever had in my eyes! It was sensitive to light and it hurt badly. Even touching it knocked me to my knees. As I got ready for the meeting and was going toward the elevator, I saw one of the men who ministered at the meetings. He was one of the main speakers so I asked him to pray for my eye.

At the conference, many miracles were occurring. Deaf ears were opened, blind eyes were restored, and more. He asked me what was wrong and I told him.

He said, "Well, let's take care of that right now."

He put his hands on the sides of my head and put his thumb right on that painful eye. I thought I would pass out the pain was so bad. Then, he pressed on my eye even harder. This felt even worse than when I just touched it in the morning!

"Oh, so we have a tumor there," he said.

As he pressed on my eye, a gray looking mass came out of my right eye and started running down my cheek. He took his handkerchief and cleaned it off my face. He threw his handkerchief in the trash can and said, "That takes care of that. Now let's go in and enjoy the meeting!"

My eye was instantly healed! All the pain was gone and the redness and swelling were also gone.

I sat near him at the meeting. As the first speaker of the night brought up people to share their healing testimonies, he was sitting beside me saying, "Thank You, Jesus; thank You, Father" under his breath the whole time.

He was so happy and thankful about the things God was doing at the meetings. God had just performed a significant miracle through him when he prayed for me. He was still so excited about the things God was doing for other people through other ministers. His attitude of thankfulness and humility surprised me. If God healed someone like that when I prayed for them, I would want everyone to know about it. God taught me through his example that it's not about me and what people think of me; it's about Jesus and what they think of Him.

It's not about me and what people think of me; it's about Jesus and what people think of Him.

One of my friends is a painting contractor. He told me that his business has become much more profitable as he put into practice some of the things he learned from our sessions.

3 John verse 2 says, *"Beloved, I pray that you may prosper in all things and be in health, just as your soul prospers."*

My friend needed to see more prospering in his business. He realized he needed help setting boundaries for his business so he could keep more of the profit. He had a tendency to let his clients and crews take advantage of him.

When the customer changed the scope of work and the job took longer because of the change, he was reluctant to charge them more for the extra work. When crews were scheduled on a job and they didn't finish it right, he went in and cleaned up after them or paid someone else to do it instead of requiring the crew to take care of their own mess. He was nervous about holding people accountable because he thought he might lose new jobs from the clients if he charged them more money for the extra items. He also thought he would lose the crew if he required that they do more than they wanted to do.

The lesson for him boiled down to holding other people accountable in the same way he was held accountable. As he worked through some of his personal cognitive distortions and learned new communications skills, his company became more profitable and the business became stronger. Clients, as it turned out, want to have good communication from a contractor. They don't really have trouble paying a fair price for additional items that have to be done on a job.

Prayer...

Lord Jesus, thank You for giving me a teachable spirit so I can learn from You in every situation. Thank You for Your grace and favor so I can prosper in all things just as my soul prospers. In the name of Jesus Christ, Amen.

Chapter 7 - A New Day

A number of years ago, I was invited to preach at a large church at the Sunday morning service. After the service, a lady came up and said, "God told me to give you something."

"Ok," I said, not really knowing where this would go.

She told me that a few years earlier, she was out shopping and was strongly attracted to a ring in a jewelry store.

"It was amazing!" she said. It had diamonds in the center and rubies surrounded them so it looked like a new variety of flower. She asked God why that ring had grabbed her attention and she asked God if she could buy it.

God said, "Yes, but the ring is not for you to keep. You can enjoy it until I tell you who you are supposed to give it to."

When she heard me share that morning, God told her to give the ring to me.

"This ring is for your wife," she said.

About twelve years later, I met Barbara and I knew the ring was for her. God heard the cry of my heart and set things in motion so a stranger would give me a special ring. That ring was a symbol of God's promise to me that He would bring me a wife. I thought about selling that ring several times during those years because I needed the money. The ring was worth thousands of dollars. As a minister, I didn't think I had enough money at times. But I kept the ring. Each time I looked at it, I reminded myself of God's promise. Barbara has been such a blessing to me and I can't imagine my life without her. If I had not already been married to Barbara, I would ask her to marry me right now. Barbara is going to share the story of how we met from her perspective.

Barbara…

One night, I was at a church and Chuck was the speaker. He shared his testimony and I remember thinking, "Lord please forgive me if I ever complain about my problems again! My problems are so small compared to what he's been through. I will never complain again!"

I was a single mom with two daughters and working as a bookkeeper. My car was on its last legs. Actually, so was I. I needed a lot of healing in my life and I was very impressed with Chuck's testimony. God had worked so many miracles in his life. He had already come through more trouble than I could imagine. I had seen God work in my life. I had seen God help me in all kinds of areas, but nothing came close to the way God had come through for Chuck.

Before Chuck and I started seeing each other, the church I attended had a financial seminar. They taught a model of living on 80% of your income, tithing 10%, and saving 10%.

I told the Lord, "I really want to do that."

I used to be an all or nothing kind of person; if I couldn't give 10%, I would give nothing. One of my friends helped me see the error of that, so I started giving God a smaller percentage on a regular basis. My goal was to give 10%. I was slowly working my way up to that goal by giving what I could from each paycheck. As I started to honor God with my giving, He started to bless me. I was getting to the goal of giving 10% faster than I thought I would.

I met Chuck as I was in this process. I had heard Chuck's testimony six years earlier at church but I didn't meet him then. I heard Chuck would be speaking at church again and I really wanted to hear him. This time, I went up and talked to him after he shared his testimony, which I never would have done previously because I am a shy person. I joke about being a "Slow mover." But the truth is, I was just shy. We really hit it off as we talked after church and decided to meet again the next night. We talked for three hours the next night and started dating. After six weeks, we knew we would be married.

I told my sister, "I am madly in love."

She said, "You can't be madly in love in six weeks!"

"Ok," I said. "I'm madly infatuated then. Ha!"

We knew deep down that God was doing something special by bringing us together.

As we dated, I found myself stretched financially. I couldn't keep up with my new social life and keep giving to the Lord, too. So, I quit giving.

Before too long, I started to get depressed and it wouldn't go away. I had a prayer partner and she agreed to pray with me every day to lift the depression. I also got sick. I had one sinus infection after another. I would take antibiotics. As soon as I was finished with the prescription, another sinus infection would flare up. This happened over and over and over. I was praying about it and the Lord took me to **Malachi 3:7**...

> *Ever since the days of your ancestors, you have scorned my decrees and failed to obey them. Now return to me, and I will return to you," says the LORD of Heaven's Armies. "But you ask, 'How can we return when we have never gone away?'*

I felt so far away from God. It was amazing to me that He brought me to this specific passage. I remember saying, "Lord, I *do* feel far away from you, how can I return to you?"

And He said, "Keep reading."

> **Malachi 3: 8-12**, *Should people cheat God? Yet you have cheated me! But you ask, 'What do you mean? When did we ever cheat you?' You have cheated me of the tithes and offerings due to me. You are under a curse, for your whole nation has been cheating me. Bring all the tithes into the storehouse so there will be enough food in my Temple. If you do, says the LORD of Heaven's Armies, I will open the*

*windows of heaven for you. I will pour out a
blessing so great you won't have enough room
to take it in! Try it! Put me to the test! Your
crops will be abundant, for I will guard them
from insects and disease. Your grapes will not
fall from the vine before they are ripe, says
the LORD of Heaven's Armies. Then all nations
will call you blessed, for your land will be such a
delight, says the LORD of Heaven's Armies.*

This passage hit me powerfully. In the last sentence, I crossed out "You" in my Bible and put "Barbara," and yet... I remember thinking, "Lord, what does this have to do with depression?"

So I didn't do it. Another couple of months went by before I finally realized that God wouldn't give me step two until I had obeyed step one.

It was close to August 1 and the depression and sickness had been going on for many months.

I decided I'd better listen to what God was telling me. My job had always been hourly. I didn't have a salary; I only got paid for the hours I worked. The business was slow and I wasn't making very much money. I was afraid. I didn't know if I would have enough to support my two children and myself, but I took a step of faith and obedience and gave 10% of what came in to the Lord.

That August, the first month I tithed, I made enough money to pay all my bills plus $200. And I got well. And my depression went away. Even though Chuck and I knew within six weeks of meeting each other that we would be married, we had a check in our spirits. The Lord had not given us the go ahead to get married. When I made the decision to go ahead and obey God, we both got peace in our hearts that it was ok for us to get married.

What I realized was that, when I met Chuck, I took God off the throne of my life and put Chuck on it. The Lord wanted me to know that a man would not rescue me from my financial problems. God wanted me to know that HE was my provider. **Malachi 4:2** spoke to me at the same time that God was revealing this truth to me...

But for you who fear my name, the Sun of Righteousness will rise with healing in his wings. And you will go free, leaping with joy like calves let out to pasture."

The Lord healed me when I put Him back on the throne. If God's not on the throne of your life, you can expect trouble with finances, among other things. I want to encourage you right now to turn your heart toward God. It doesn't matter what has gone on in the past for you and it doesn't matter what is going on right now; God cares deeply for you. He is able to help you in the same way He helped me. He really wants to help you if you will let Him.

I John 1:9 says, *"If we confess our sins He is faithful and just to forgive us of all our sins and cleanse us from all unrighteousness."*

If you have put someone or something before God, please pray this prayer with me...

Dear Lord, please forgive me for putting _____ before You. I don't want anything standing between You and me. I don't want anything to hinder our relationship. You said in Your word that if I confess my sins, You are faithful and just to forgive me of my sins and to cleanse me from all unrighteousness. I ask this in Jesus name, Amen. Thank You, Lord!

Chapter 8 - I Remember

I remember one of the first lessons God taught me about money. I was at church and I was a brand new believer. I wanted to put five dollars in the offering plate but all I had was a ten-dollar bill. It was the only money I had in the world! I was going to put the ten-dollar bill in and take out change. Why not? I was still giving half of everything I had. That was pretty good, right?

The Holy Spirit Whispered to me, "Do you trust me?"

The Holy Spirit whispered to me, "Do you trust Me?"

I responded and said, "Yes, kind of."

I resisted, wouldn't you? The Holy Spirit kept whispering the same thing over and over. I didn't hear an audible voice, but I felt the thought rise up from deep inside me. I knew it wasn't my thought because giving the entire ten dollars was the last thing on my mind!

Finally, the offering plate came and I put the ten-dollar bill in the plate. But I was still holding on to the bill. The usher said, "You have to let go of it."

I finally did. As I was leaving Church that morning, one of the businessmen in the church came up to me and shook my hand. I felt a folded-up piece of paper in his hand. As we finished shaking hands, he released the paper into my hand.

He turned and walked off as though nothing out of the ordinary had happened. Upon opening my hand, I found a fifty-dollar bill! My jaw hit the floor. I don't think I had ever seen a fifty-dollar bill before.

I heard that same small voice inside me say, "Just be faithful to do what I ask you to do and I will take care of you. "

I remember taking my daughter shopping at Wal-Mart when she was about five years old. At one point, she wanted me to buy her something I didn't think I should buy her.

I said, "No."

Well, at that time in her life, my daughter thought that throwing fits was a good way to get what she wanted. She threw herself on the floor at Wal-Mart right in the middle of the aisle and started crying and screaming. Very soon, a group of people gathered around her to find out what was wrong. I stood in the circle of onlookers.

I could hear comments like, "I wonder where her parents are?" "Is she hurt? Did she hurt herself?" "What's going on?" "What's wrong?"

The people around me didn't know I was her dad because I was just watching the scene as everyone else was. After a few minutes, she stopped crying and looked around. When she caught my eye, I asked her, "Are you finished?"

A Defining Moment!

She nodded her head, got up, and we walked out of there. My daughter never had another public temper tantrum like that again. Later, she told me that it was a defining moment for her. She realized the fit she threw did not get her the result she wanted. She said she felt embarrassed and did not want to feel like that again.

The people probably thought I was crazy or cruel to stand there letting my daughter make a scene. The result is what counted. My daughter changed her behavior because she didn't get what she wanted by that old behavior.

I love the saying, "If you want to get a different result, you have to be willing to take a different action." It is dysfunctional to do the same bad behavior over and over, hoping for a different result.

I recall shopping in King Soopers one day and watching a lady put a young girl in a grocery cart. The girl started screaming. The immediate reaction from the mom was, "Shut up or I'll take you out to the car and give you something to cry about."

Then, the mom must have thought better about her initial response and asked, "Honey, what's wrong?"

"This thing is pinching my leg," the five-year old said. The metal cart was physically hurting her. It was not a temper tantrum as the mom had first thought. Parenting can be so challenging. Just when you think one lesson is figured out, another situation pops up and a new solution is required. I'm so glad the mom pressed in to find out what the problem really was before punishing the little girl for what she had thought was a temper tantrum.

I had the privilege of meeting Joni Erikson Tada at Craig Hospital. When she was a teenager, she broke her neck in a diving accident. She had become paralyzed from the neck down and needed help to do the simplest things. She went through severe depression and was angry at God for not having healed her immediately. She wanted to help people; she wanted to encourage people but felt helpless because her body was now broken.

God is not restricted by our limitations.

One day, she wanted to draw a picture. The only way she could draw the picture was to hold the pencil or paint brush in her mouth. She learned to draw beautifully even though she could only hold the brush in her mouth. She gave Craig Hospital one of her pictures. Every time I look at it, I am reminded that God is not restricted by our limitations.

When something is not working in our bodies, God can work around that obstacle and help us arrive at the same goal another way. God has more options to help us succeed than we can imagine.

Although Joni's body may be broken, she has a strong spirit and faith in the same God that I love. It helps me to remember that **God is not looking for perfect people; He's just looking for people who are available to be used for His purposes.**

Kathryn Kuhlman said it this way: "God's not looking for golden or silver vessels. He's just looking for yielded vessels."

Your mess can become your message. My pain was what God used to help me understand my purpose.

One day, I took Barb out to lunch at a restaurant not too far from her office. As we were being seated, a man came up to our table. He told me that I had shared an emotional word picture with him twenty-eight years before and he never forgot it. An emotional word picture is like a parable that has elements in it that the listener can easily relate to. He briefly told us what the word picture was and how significant it was to him. We were so glad he came over! After we shook hands, he went back to his table.

Barbara asked me, "Who was that?"   I didn't remember him but he had certainly remembered the word picture! It is so encouraging to know that if I am just obedient to say what God tells me to say, He will do the rest.

Prayer…

Father God, in the name of Jesus, please help us to be aware of Your still, small voice as we move forward, doing what You have called us to do. Help us to recognize the spiritual conclusions that our actions will bring as we minister for the glory of Your Kingdom. Thank You for using us for Your glory. In the name of Jesus we pray, Amen.

Chapter 9 - Right Now

If you look around at the state of affairs in the world, it seems as though all hell is breaking loose. I believe we are seeing a dramatic increase in demonic activity because the enemy knows that it won't be long now until all *Heaven* breaks loose.

I met an Iranian pastor at a Missions conference I spoke at in 2015. He told me that the Muslim people are hungry for God. At one service, he asked the congregation, "How many of you have seen Jesus in a vision or a dream?"

Thirty out of the thirty-five people said they had. Times have changed! Jesus is revealing Himself to the Muslim people. In the past, people tried to evangelize Muslims by presenting evidence to them about the truth of the Bible. They also identified various problems with the Koran. In the past, Muslims responded by arguing with the people who confronted them. Now they just want to hear about Jesus.

"Don't give us arguments to pull us away from Islam. Just tell us about Jesus!"

They already have had a lot of experience with Muslim traditions and they see how broken it is. They simply want us to tell them the truth about Jesus so they can be free. The pastor invited me to speak at their church and a number of people accepted Jesus. The pastor said that some of them had been waiting a year to make the decision for Christ because of the high price they have to pay to become a Christian. They give up their families to follow Jesus. Some of them even give up their lives.

God does not make mistakes. Do you feel like a big mistake sometimes? I've got good news for you: God loves you and He has wonderful plans for your life.

Jeremiah 29:11 says, *For I know the plans I have for you," says the LORD. "They are plans for good and not for disaster, to give you a future and a hope."*

Have you ever wondered why you are here on this Earth? We are here so that God the Father can love us. God loves us so much, He sent His only Son Jesus to die for us so we could be part of His family. When you accept Jesus into your heart, you become part of God's family. You also become part of the reward Jesus died to win. You were born to love God and glorify Him forever. You were born to become part of His family and grow up into the maturity and fullness of Jesus. You were born to know God personally and honor Him in everything you do.

Sometimes life doesn't seem to go very well because we become so involved in our own problems and living our own lives. The truth is that God placed us here so that He could love us and we could learn to love Him too. His purpose for us is that we will live our lives with His manifest presence around us all the time.

Our purpose is to live a presence-filled life. We are to live with His presence evident in every area of our lives. We can know Him and the power of His resurrection. We can have Jesus walk with us no matter where we go, even to the ends of the earth. We can learn everything we need to know from the Holy Spirit and the Word of God, the Bible. We can complete all the good deeds God has prepared for us to do.

I once attended a Kathryn Kuhlman meeting when I was young. The presence of God was powerful!

"Don't touch the glory," she said.

What she meant was, "Don't take credit for these great miracles. God is the one who heals and He deserves all the glory."

When I was in my early twenties, I had the same kind of healing anointing Kathryn Kuhlman had but I abused it. I didn't know how to handle it. I had meetings set up for a year in Canada. All the Crusades and radio broadcasts were lined up. There were five security guards that walked me onto the platform because the crowds were so eager to get something from me. I let it go to my head... I became proud and because of that, the Lord took it all away from me. He told me to go to Mexico because he wanted to humble me.

"Go to Old Mexico and minister there," God said.

"What?" I heard myself say. But I knew it was God speaking to me.

So I told the coordinator what God told me to do. The coordinator became angry! The people who had set up the crusades and radio broadcasts were furious because I had thrown a wrench in all the plans they had made, but I had to walk away.

I still recall God telling me, "You do not touch the glory." God showed me that we are the conduit, not the source. I'm so glad I listened to God and walked away instead of trying to press ahead in my own strength.

When you begin doing what God has called you to do, you begin experiencing the fullness of Christ. You can either get puffed up or you can press more deeply into God. God wants to set us on fire so that we become radical people of faith who are not afraid to share Jesus Christ with whomever we encounter. God wants us to live our lives burning passionately for Him.

Billy Sunday said, "If you get on fire for God, people will come from miles around just to watch you burn."

I've met some people who were afraid to share Jesus because they were afraid people would then expect them to be perfect. The good news is that God gives us all the grace and strength we need to do the things He asks us to do. None of us are perfect.

Your story of how God saved you and how He is working in your life right now is one of the most powerful things you have to share with people. No one wants to hear a bunch of religious talk. People want to have real friendships with real people who make mistakes. People want friends who are honest enough to talk about the hard things in their lives. We don't have time to fake it and pretend things are fine when they are not. Everyone wants to talk to someone who is willing to open their heart and share at a deep level.

People want to see Jesus. They want to see walking and talking examples of what God's Word can do in our lives. Your story about how you got from where you were to where you are now is a vital! People don't want just to *hear* about Jesus, they want to *see* Jesus. They want to see our changed lives. They want to see God's love in us. We have the opportunity to walk in love with each other. That is what will attract people to God more than anything.

We are serving a God Who knows no defeat. Maybe you are feeling defeated as you read my story because you need a miracle and you haven't seen one happening in your life. You are reading about the miracles that have happened to me and some of the people I know. However, it's kind of a good news/bad news situation. The good news is that I have experienced so many miracles personally, no one can convince me they don't happen. They are real! The bad news is that your mind may doubt God will do a miracle for you.

If you are reading this book and need a miracle, you are in the best place in the world to receive a miracle. The presence of the Lord is here and He will meet you at the point of your need. God knows exactly what you need. However, God wants you to ask Him for those things.

I want to encourage you first to receive Jesus Christ as your personal Lord and Savior. If you've never asked Christ to come into your heart and your life, do that right now. Don't take the chance of missing the most wonderful Friend you could ever have. You certainly don't want to miss the chance to be in God's family and live with Him forever. Will you open the door of your heart to Jesus and ask Him to come in?

Revelation 3:20 says, *"Look! I stand at the door and knock. If you hear My voice and open the door, I will come in..."*

Have you ever seen the famous picture of Jesus standing at the door knocking? If you look closely at that picture, you will see there is no doorknob on the outside. **The door represents your heart. You have to open** the door of your heart from the inside. **You have to let God in**. God is not a boundary-buster.

He is not going to push His way in and say, "I know you need Me so I'm going to come in whether you want Me to or not." Jesus waits for you to invite Him into your life.

God does not need you to clean up your act before He comes to you. The Bible does not say, "If you get your life straightened out, if you get your life cleaned up, then I'll come in". All you have to do is to be willing to open that door.

This was so encouraging to me when I asked Jesus into my life because I couldn't fix all my problems by myself. I needed God to come into my heart and change me from the inside out. As soon as God gave me a new heart, the other things that needed to be changed in my life began to change. That is how God works. He doesn't expect us to fix ourselves. He knows we can't. He also knows we can't fix other people.

The Lord told me one time, "You catch 'them and I'll clean 'them!"

I'm a fisherman so I love that! It's none of my business to clean up and fix the people that come to Him. That's God's business. One of my favorite promises is in **Philippians 1:6** where it says that *"God will keep doing the good work He started to do in your life until it's finished."* Are you ready for God to start a good work in you? Are you ready to receive Jesus into your heart? Pray this prayer out loud with me...

Heavenly Father, I come to You right now. You said in Your Word that if I would confess my sins, that You are faithful and just to forgive me of my sins and to cleanse me from all unrighteousness. Lord Jesus, I

confess that I'm a sinner. I open the door of my heart

right now and ask You to come in and be my Lord and

Savior. Wash my sins away by the blood of Jesus

Christ. I pray this prayer by faith and from this moment

on I will live for Jesus Christ. The old things will pass

away and all things will become new. In the name of

Jesus Christ, Amen.

Go to the Bible for Truth. Build your life and foundation on what God says.

The following verses confirm that you are saved. We do not base our lives on emotional or even intellectual arguments. As Christians, we go to the Bible for truth. We build our foundation and our lives on what God says. We learn from the Holy Spirit and we purpose to agree with what God says. If God says that this is what I should do to be saved, then that is what I must do.

Romans 10:9-10 *If you openly declare that Jesus is Lord and believe in your heart that God raised Him from the dead, you* will be saved. *10 For it is by believing in your heart that you are made right with God, and it is by openly declaring your faith that you are saved.*

Ephesians 2:8-9 *God saved you by his grace when you believed. And you can't take credit for this; it is a gift from God. Salvation is not a reward for the good things we have done, so none of us can boast about it.*

Philippians 1:6 *And I am certain that God, who began the good work within you, will continue His work until it is finally finished on the day when Christ Jesus returns.*

Thank You, Father, that Your word is true and we can trust You to do what You've promised to do. In the name of Jesus Christ, Amen.

My prayer is that my life story has blessed you and helped you see that what you are experiencing is not necessarily uncommon, healing is available. You have read my story and now it is time to do the work so you can be healed, delivered, and set free from those things that are keeping you from being able to move forward in your life.

May God bless you on this journey of life as you come to know Him more and walk in the levels of healing and excellence He created just for you.

God bless you!

Pastor Chuck

Skills for Life

Skills for Life Introduction

Some people have great advice and others do not. It is important who you listen to. You have to decide whether you should accept someone's counsel or not. The Life Skills I share in this book will work for you because they work for everyone who learns how to use them. The Bible is the foundational element for these skills.

The following statements are some of the reasons the Life Skills in this book are important for us to learn. In this section of the book, many passages from the Bible are included. **The way to work through this is to ask the Holy Spirit to teach you as you read, and then meditate on the scriptures that are identified.**

1. God wants every person in the world to be in His family. **(John 3:16)**
2. God determined that love would be the way He would draw all men to Himself. **(Romans 5:8)**
3. He chose to partner with us and He gave us the Holy Spirit to live in us so we could love people the way He does. **(John 14:25-27) (Acts 1:8)**
4. God says that loving our neighbors is the way the world will know that we love God. **(I John 4:19-21) (I John 3:17-18)**

5. Loving each other as Christians is the way that people will know that Jesus is God. **(John 17:22-23)**

John 3:16 *For this is how God loved the world: He gave his one and only Son, so that everyone who believes in him will not perish but have eternal life.*

Romans 5:8 *But God showed his great love for us by sending Christ to die for us while we were still sinners.*

John 14:25-27 *I am telling you these things now while I am still with you. But when the Father sends the Advocate as my representative—that is, the Holy Spirit—he will teach you everything and will remind you of everything I have told you. "I am leaving you with a gift—peace of mind and heart. And the peace I give is a gift the world cannot give. So don't be troubled or afraid.*

Acts 1:8 *But you will receive power when the Holy Spirit comes*

upon you

I John 4:19-21 *We love each other because he loved us first. If someone says, "I love God," but hates a fellow believer, that person is a liar; for if we don't love people we can see, how can we love God, whom we cannot see? And he has given us this command: Those who love God must also love their fellow believers.*

I John 3:17-18 *If someone has enough money to live well and sees a brother or sister in need but shows no compassion—how can God's love be in that person?*

John 17:22-23 *I have given them the glory you gave Me, so they may be one as We are one. I am in them and You are in Me. May* *they experience such perfect unity that the world will know that You sent Me and that You love them as much as You love Me.*

I have counseled people for 40 years. The following Life Skills are the ones I have taught the most. We develop better skills as we practice them. Practice does not make us perfect, but it does make us better! These skills are like tools you can carry in your tool belt. When I run into a problem, I pull out the right tool and use it to work on the problem before me. I may not solve the problem perfectly the first time, but as I use these skills, I improve. As I practice these skills, I find that they help me to live my life with joy, hope, courage, and peace.

I am only summarizing the Life Skills in this book. There are CD's and DVD's of each Life Skill available on line at www.chucklewisministries.com I would love to hear from you as God transforms your life. The ministry website has an email link so you can send me a letter.

Every promise from God is like a contract. When you say, "Yes Father, I agree with You," you are signing your name at the bottom of a contract written by God. One step at a time, one "Yes" to God at a time. That's all it takes! In the following sections, I will list some verses and I encourage you to ask the Holy Spirit to teach you as you meditate on them.

Interactions: These activities can be done for each of the Life Skills. We learn best when we interact with what we are learning. Choose one or more of the interactions and write down your thoughts. If you are working on this with another person or a small group, share some of these thoughts with them.

- Ask God to help you understand one of the verses from the Life Skill lesson. Read the verse again and take some notes about what you think God is saying to you.
- You might also make a journal entry about what you think or feel related to one of these verses.
- Will this Life Skill work for Christians and non-Christians? Why or why not?
- What does loving myself and loving other people have to do with this Life Skill?
- How does this Life Skill relate to honor and respect?
- Write out the verses from the Life Skill lesson on 3 by 5 cards and carry them with you. Pull them out and meditate on them whenever you have time and wherever you are. Stick verses on the mirror so you can meditate on them as you get ready for the day. Tape them on the refrigerator, the coffeemaker, and even the TV remote.

Life Skill index

1. Time Outs

Most people may think time-outs are just for kids. But have you observed as I have, that often, grownups act like children and they need to take a time-out?

"Ouch!" I know it may be hard to hear that but we are all in the same boat. I have needed to take time outs in my life just as you have. When you get angry, it is possible to say things that are unkind to those around you. You can damage others with your words. As a result, you damage the relationship you have with them because of your angry words.

When we speak, we can either contribute to the conversation or contaminate it. Contributing is encouraging the other person, understanding them, and growing closer. Contaminating is bringing negative comments into the conversation which make it harder for us to get along. Contributing helps the relationship; contaminating pollutes it. So as a commercial reminded us. "Give a hoot! Don't pollute!" Sometimes taking a few minutes away from the person you are talking to is the best decision you can make. You don't want to make things worse with angry words. Once those words are out, they cannot be taken back. (See Appendix A for more information about the time-out process.)

Scriptures for Learners

Proverbs 18:21 *The tongue can bring death or life; those who love to talk will reap the consequences.*

Matthew 21:21 *Then Jesus told them, "I tell you the truth, if you have faith and don't doubt, you can do things like this and much more. You can even say to this mountain, 'May you be lifted up and thrown into the sea,' and it will happen.*

James 3:3-6 *We can make a large horse go wherever we want by means of a small bit in its mouth. And a small rudder makes a huge ship turn wherever the pilot chooses to go, even though the winds are strong. In the same way, the tongue is a small thing that makes grand speeches. But a tiny spark can set a great forest on fire. And among all the parts of the body, the tongue is a flame of fire. It is a whole world of wickedness, corrupting your entire body. It can set your whole life on fire, for it is set on fire by hell itself.*

2. Cognitive Distortions

The term *Cognitive Distortions* is a clinical and professional way to identify "stinking thinking". It is so easy for us to become negative and selfish in our thoughts. The good news about cognitive distortions is that you can let them go. You can replace them with positive, encouraging, and truth-filled beliefs. The Bible says, "As a man thinks in his heart, so is he" **(Prov 23:7)**. Our thoughts become beliefs and the beliefs we develop determine how we talk, how we understand other people, and how we live. What we believe and how we talk to ourselves (self-talk) are critical elements to how we react and feel.

Our normal self-talk is what we learned growing up or heard other people saying to us. This self-talk can be changed and that is good news. We can replace the beliefs and self-talk that are negative and harmful to us and our goals, with self-talk that is true and positive. If a house is built on a faulty foundation, it will fall. The bad foundation has to be rebuilt before the solid and true foundation can be placed on it. **Our self-talk must be developed with the Word of God as our primary source.** (See Appendix B for a list of specific Cognitive Distortions. Appendix C is a worksheet that may help also.)

Scriptures for Learners

Romans 12:1-2 *And so, dear brothers and sisters, I plead with you to give your bodies to God because of all he has done for you. Let them be a living and holy sacrifice—the kind he will find acceptable. This is truly the way to worship him. Don't copy the behavior and customs of this world, but let God transform you into a new person by changing the way you think. Then you will learn to know God's will for you, which is good and pleasing and perfect.*

2 Corinthians 1:20 *For all of God's promises have been fulfilled in Christ with a resounding "Yes!" And through Christ, our "Amen" (which means "Yes") ascends to God for his glory.*

2 Corinthians 10:4-5 *We use God's mighty weapons, not worldly weapons, to knock down the strongholds of human reasoning and to destroy false arguments. We destroy every proud obstacle that keeps people from knowing God. We capture their rebellious thoughts and teach them to obey Christ.*

Phil 2:5 *You must have the same attitude that Christ Jesus had.*

3. Speaker/Listener Technique

Have you ever watched two people talking to each other at the same time? When I see that, I wonder, "Which one is listening?" It would be better to talk to a wall than to someone who is talking at the same time as you are. Many businesses and professional people use the Speaker/Listener technique so they are certain that they are communicating with the clients they serve. This skill is helpful as we work to avoid dysfunctional conflicts and also to resolve conflict if it has already begun. There are rules we can follow that make even conflict situations manageable. (See Appendix D for some practical guidelines to use the Speaker/Listener technique.)

Scriptures for learners

Matthew 13:9 *Anyone with ears to hear should listen and understand.*

1 Corinthians 10:13 *The temptations in your life are no different from what others experience. And God is faithful. He will not allow the temptation to be more than you can stand. When you are tempted, he will show you a way out so that you can endure.*

Ephesians 4:29 *Don't use foul or abusive language. Let everything you say be good and helpful, so that your words will be an encouragement to those who hear them.*

4. Filters

We develop our unique perspective and worldview through our life filters. Those filters are formed from the different experiences we have had. An oil filter on a car strains out dirt and contaminates. The filter protects the engine so it can work the way it was designed to work. When we have good filters for our life in place, we can operate at our best. Good life filters help us strain out harmful and dangerous things so that we can function the way we were designed to function. Most of us did not grow up with good life filters. We need to identify exactly what our filters are so that we can replace them with positive ones.

Another way to look at this dynamic is to realize that if the truth will set you free, then a lie will bind you. Negative life filters are often simply lies that bind us in some way. The good news is that we can be free from all those negative life filters. It may take time to be released from some of them, but every journey begins with a single step. There is not one filter that is too difficult for God. All the negative filters, those lies you've believed, did not come from God. The devil is the one who comes to kill, steal, and destroy. The best way to overcome a lie is to receive the truth.

Scriptures for learners

Proverbs 23:7 *For as he thinks in his heart, so is he.*

John 8:32 *So if the Son sets you free, you are truly free.*

John 8:36 *If the Son therefore shall make you free, ye shall be free indeed.*

5. How to Manage Conflict

Managing conflict has a lot to do with learning to *respond* to a situation instead of simply *reacting* to it. Reacting is easy-- just do what you feel like doing when facing a challenging situation. Often those harmful reactions fall into the category of bad behavior. It is easy to do the wrong things; they come naturally. We have to practice doing the right things if we want to manage conflict well. The following questions will help you look at how you manage conflict:

1. How do you deal with conflict? What happened the last time you had a conflict? How did that work for you? You are only responsible for yourself and how you respond. The other person is responsible for themself because you cannot control others.

2. Do you avoid conflicts like the plague? If you do, there is a reason for it. You have a filter in place that tells you to operate that way.

3. How did your family deal with conflict growing up? If your family dealt with conflict the wrong way, it is not surprising that you do, too.

One of the keys for managing conflict well is to honor and respect the people in your life. **The more we honor and respect each other, the less unresolved conflict we will have.**

Scriptures for Learners

Matthew 18:15-16 *If another believer sins against you, go privately and point out the offense. If the other person listens and confesses it, you have won that person back. But if you are unsuccessful, take one or two others with you and go back again, so that everything you say may be confirmed by two or three witnesses.*

Galatians 5:26 *Let us not become conceited, or provoke one another, or be jealous of one another.*

Ephesians 4:26-27 *And don't sin by letting anger control you." Don't let the sun go down while you are still angry, for anger gives a foothold to the devil.*

6. Emotional Word Pictures

When we talk with someone, we want them to understand what we are trying to say. Emotional word pictures are powerful methods to help to clarify our intention. An emotional word picture is a communication tool that uses a story or object to activate, simultaneously, the emotions and intellect of a person. The right side and left side of the brain process information differently.

Emotional word pictures engage both sides of the brain at the same time. They cause the person to experience our words and not merely hear them. The most effective emotional word pictures are the ones the person you are talking with can relate to. The purposes for using emotional word pictures are:

1. To clarify a thought or feeling;

2. To move you to a deeper level of intimacy;

3. To praise or encourage someone;

4. To lovingly correct someone.

Use the tangible to describe the intangible. You can create emotional word pictures from nature, animals, weather, mountains, water, everyday objects, imaginary stories, and even past memories or experiences. Use this life skill often!

If I am talking to an electrician, I will use an example that has something to do with electricity. A plumber will understand it better if I use an emotional word picture related to plumbing.

Scriptures for Learners

Psalms 1 *Oh, the joys of those who do not follow the advice of the wicked, or stand around with sinners, or join in with mockers. But they delight in the law of the LORD, meditating on it day and night.*
They are like trees planted along the riverbank, bearing fruit each season. Their leaves never wither, and they prosper in all they do. But not the wicked! They are like worthless chaff, scattered by the wind. They will be condemned at the time of judgment. Sinners will have no place among the godly. For the LORD watches over the path of the godly, but the path of the wicked leads to destruction.

Isaiah 40:31 *But those who trust in the LORD will find new strength. They will soar high on wings like eagles. They will run and not grow weary. They will walk and not faint.*

Luke 13:18-21 *Then Jesus said, "What is the Kingdom of God like? How can I illustrate it? It is like a tiny mustard seed that a man planted in a garden; it grows and becomes a tree, and the birds make nests in its branches." He also asked, "What else is the Kingdom of God like? [21] It is like the yeast a woman used in making bread. Even though she put only a little yeast in three measures of flour, it permeated every part of the dough."*

7. Boundaries

A boundary tells us where we end and where someone else begins. It defines our responsibility and someone else's responsibility. **A boundary tells you when to say yes and when to say no so you can make clear decisions and take control of your life.**

If you grew up in a dysfunctional family, chances are you need some help understanding what appropriate boundaries are. For controlling and dominating personalities, the problem usually has to do with stepping over other people's boundaries. For passive and codependent people, the challenge has to do with setting up appropriate boundaries and then following through with a course of action to help other people respect your boundary and not step all over you.

Boundaries are something we all need. However, they are not meant to be walls that create isolation. Boundaries are more like a property line around your life.

Scriptures for Learners

Proverbs 25:28 *A person without self-control is like a city with broken-down walls.*

Matthew 7:6 *Don't waste what is holy on people who are unholy. Don't throw your pearls to pigs! They will trample the pearls, then turn and attack you.*

Ephesians 4:25 *So stop telling lies. Let us tell our neighbors the truth, for we are all parts of the same body. And don't sin by letting anger control you. Don't let the sun go down while you are still angry, for anger gives a foothold to the devil.*

8. Surface Triggers and Core Fears

Surface triggers come from past events or traumas we have had which develop into a belief system. When we make judgments or negative decisions about traumatic events from our past, it negatively impacts our present. Being rejected, made fun of, humiliated, scared, criticized, or mocked can cause core fears or surface triggers to develop. They work in the same way cognitive distortions work.

For example, if a man has a bad experience with a police officer, he may develop a belief that all police officers are bad. When I examine that belief, I discover that some police are bad but they are not all that way. Some women have had a bad experience with one man and as a result, believe all men are bad.

Surface triggers are exposed when we hear someone say something and our response is out of proportion to their comment. What they said is not what we heard because their comment triggered a past experience. We were really responding to that other past event, and not responding to what they actually said.

Scriptures for Learners

Isaiah 54:17 *No weapon turned against you will succeed. You will silence every voice raised up to accuse you. These benefits are enjoyed by the servants of the LORD; their vindication will come from me. I, the LORD, have spoken!*

2 Timothy 1:7 *For God has not given us a spirit of fear and timidity, but of power, love, and self-discipline.*

1 John 4:18 *Such love has no fear, because perfect love expels all fear. If we are afraid, it is for fear of punishment, and this shows that we have not fully experienced his perfect love.*

9. Power and Control

To take power and exert control over a situation can be either a conscious or subconscious decision. Many people only feel comfortable if they are making all the decisions and controlling the situation. They consciously control the people and events around them. Power and control can also be a subconscious drive. Low self-esteem, for example, will often motivate a person to do things subconsciously to control others. They are reacting to other powerful drives that are hidden deeply inside, such as fear or anger.

The aggressive person is one who uses power and control to get what he wants from other people. The passive person, on the other hand, is also in trouble because they make it a practice to bury their anger unsuccessfully. **We are not to be aggressive and we are not to be passive. God wants us to live right in the middle**, which is in being assertive. Assertive people say what they mean and mean what they say. Jesus is a great example of an assertive person. You never had to guess with Jesus; He told it like it was.

Scriptures for learners

Acts 1:8 *But you will receive power when the Holy Spirit comes upon you. And you will be my witnesses, telling people about me everywhere—in Jerusalem, throughout Judea, in Samaria, and to the ends of the earth.*

2 Timothy 3:1-5 *You should know this, Timothy, that in the last days there will be very difficult times. For people will love only themselves and their money. They will be boastful and proud, scoffing at God, disobedient to their parents, and ungrateful. They will consider nothing sacred. They will be unloving and unforgiving; they will slander others and have no self-control. They will be cruel and hate what is good. They will betray their friends, be reckless, be puffed up with pride, and love pleasure rather than God. They will act religious, but they will reject the power that could make them godly. Stay away from people like that!*

2 Peter 1:3-7 *By his divine power, God has given us everything we need for living a godly life. We have received all of this by coming to know him, the one who called us to himself by means of his marvelous glory and excellence. And because of his glory and excellence, he has given us great and precious promises. These are the promises that enable you to share his divine nature and escape the world's corruption caused by human desires. In view of all this, make every effort to respond to God's promises. Supplement your faith with a generous provision of moral excellence, and moral excellence with knowledge, and knowledge with self-control, and self-control with patient endurance, and patient endurance with godliness, and godliness with brotherly affection, and brotherly affection with love for everyone.*

10. Adult Strategies

Adult strategies have to do with operating from an adult position of maturity and not from the immature nature of a child. The child position is described as operating out of your flesh or just doing what comes naturally. **Galatians 5:22** has a list that describes how adults operate. *But the fruit of the Spirit is love, joy, peace, patience, kindness, goodness, faithfulness, gentleness and self-control.*

Life skills are like oil on a bearing; the bearings work better with oil. We're not going to talk a lot about how to live from a child position that comes naturally. **I don't need to take notes to remember how to do things wrong**. We all have a sin nature that makes it easy to be selfish and to live our lives full of pride. If we feed the spirit, we can walk in the benefits of the spirit. If we feed the flesh, we will reap the drama of the flesh. (See Appendix F for some adult strategies you can use.)

Scriptures for Learners

I Corinthians 13 *If I could speak all the languages of earth and of angels, but didn't love others, I would only be a noisy gong or a clanging cymbal. If I had the gift of prophecy, and if I understood all of God's secret plans and possessed all knowledge, and if I had such faith that I could move mountains, but didn't love others, I would be nothing. If I gave everything I have to the poor and even sacrificed my body, I could boast about it; but if I* *didn't love others, I would have gained nothing. Love is patient and kind. Love is not jealous or boastful or proud or rude. It does not demand its own way. It is not irritable, and it keeps no record of being wronged. It does not rejoice about injustice but rejoices whenever the truth wins out. Love never gives up, never loses faith, is always hopeful, and endures through every circumstance. Prophecy and speaking in unknown languages and special knowledge will become useless. But love will last forever! Now our knowledge is partial and incomplete, and even the gift of prophecy reveals only part of the whole picture! But when the time of perfection comes, these partial things will become useless. When I was a child, I spoke and thought and reasoned as a child. But when I grew up, I put away childish things. Now we see things imperfectly, like puzzling reflections in a mirror, but then we will see everything with perfect clarity. All that I know now is partial and incomplete, but then I will know everything completely, just as God now knows me completely. Three things will last forever—faith, hope, and love—and the greatest of these is love.*

11. Past, Present, and Future

God loves to turn hardship into glory. There is not one person who is too difficult for God to love and there is not one situation that is too difficult for Him to transform. No matter what situation you're in, it is simply an opportunity for you to turn that test into a testimony. **God is in the restoration business and we are the wrecks He restores.**

God wants us to be transformed by the renewing of our minds. The way we renew our mind is by meditating on the Word of God and believing what God says. When we agree with God, when we say "Yes" to Him, it changes everything. Faith begins to grow in your life because you are hearing the Word. When your faith grows, you can set down your past negative experiences and begin building good experiences now. Your future will be transformed by the decisions you make right now. It is easy to see how a problem we had in the past can impact our lives. It is also easy to see that what we believe in the present can change our future. But how can my life be impacted right now by the future?

Jeremiah 29:11 says, "For I know the plans I have for you, says the Lord. They are plans for good and not for disaster." God has good plans for your future! That gives me hope right now and that changes my present experience. What an encouraging word! What a good promise that my present experience can be joy no matter what is going on because God has good plans for my future.

Scriptures for Learners

Isaiah 61: 1-3 *The Spirit of the Sovereign LORD is upon me, for the LORD has anointed me to bring good news to the poor. He has sent me to comfort the brokenhearted and to proclaim that captives will be released and prisoners will be freed. He has sent me to tell those who mourn that the time of the LORD's favor has come, and with it, the day of God's anger against their enemies. To all who mourn in Israel, he will give a crown of beauty for ashes, a joyous blessing instead of mourning, festive praise instead of despair. In their righteousness, they will be like great oaks that the LORD has planted for his own glory.*

2 Corinthians 5:17 *This means that anyone who belongs to Christ has become a new person. The old life is gone; a new life has begun!*

Phil 3:13-14 *Forgetting the past and looking forward to what lies ahead, [14] I press on to reach the end of the race and receive the heavenly prize for which God, through Christ Jesus, is calling us.*

12. Addictions That Suppress Skills for Life

We've all encountered addictions at some level. We have either struggled personally with addictions or we have seen them played out in someone else's life. Webster's Dictionary defines addiction as, "The state of being enslaved to a habit or practice or to something that is psychologically or physically habit forming."

God has a specific destiny and plan for each person's life. One of the enemy's favorite ways to destroy that plan is through addictive behavior. What addiction or phobia does Satan try to use in your life? How does he try to oppress you? How does he distract you? Is fear what keeps you from doing what God asks you to do? God created us to be dependent upon Him. What Satan tries to do is get us to be dependent or addicted to anything else.

Our body is like a tank that holds our feelings. Your tongue is the release valve. When you can talk about Your problems, they can be put in perspective and you can deal with them in a healthy way.

Scriptures for Learners

1 Samuel 15:23 *Rebellion is as sinful as witchcraft, and stubbornness as bad as worshiping idols. So because you have rejected the command of the LORD, he has rejected you as king.*

1 Corinthians 10:13-14 *The temptations in your life are no different from what others experience. And God is faithful. He will not allow the temptation to be more than you can stand. When you are tempted, he will show you a way out so that you can endure. So, my dear friends, flee from the worship of idols.*

Colossians 3:5 *So put to death the sinful, earthly things lurking within you. Have nothing to do with sexual immorality, impurity, lust, and evil desires. Don't be greedy, for a greedy person is an idolater, worshiping the things of this world.*

13. Problem Solving

Problem solving skills enable us to feel empowered rather than like victims. As we develop this skill, we learn to exercise result thinking.

How do you solve problems? We all have large and small problems. When you start to feel stressed, it's time to identify the problems and perhaps make a list. Work on the most critical problem first. When one is taken into the emergency room, the first thing they work on is the heart and breathing. If those two things stop working, all the other things that may be wrong with you won't matter anyway. By the way, that's why God works on our hearts first, also.

What is your emotional process when you have a problem? Do you feel anxious and want to run away from the problem, or deal with it later, if at all? Procrastination is one of the biggest tools the enemy uses.

What was your experience with problem-solving growing up? How did your family solve problems when you were young? Did your parents or siblings get into conflict over problems? Did anyone ever teach you to problem solve?

Problem-solving is a skill. And like any other skill, you can learn it.

How do boundaries apply in good problem-solving skills? Most problems occur over and over because of the lack of boundaries. When we write the problem down and then look at what boundary would apply to it, often the answer is right in front of us. Taking responsibility for yourself is the foundation of good problem-solving.

Scriptures for Learners

Isaiah 43:19 *For I am about to do something new. See, I have already begun! Do you not see it? I will make a pathway through the wilderness. I will create rivers in the dry wasteland.*

Daniel 5:12 *This man Daniel, whom the king named Belteshazzar, has exceptional ability and is filled with divine knowledge and understanding. He can interpret dreams, explain riddles, and solve difficult problems. Call for Daniel, and he will tell you what the writing means.*

James 1:5 *If you need wisdom, ask our generous God, and he will give it to you. He will not rebuke you for asking.*

14. Stress

Learning to manage and reduce our stress is an important life skill. If we are stressed out and worried, we won't focus on the things God wants us to do. Each one of us has a specific purpose and a unique calling on our lives. Stress is your body's way of responding to any kind of demand. It is caused by both good and bad experiences. When people feel stressed, it is often by something going on around them. Stress is like an indicator light on your dashboard. The light on your dashboard lets you know that something is not working correctly with your car. Stress lets you know that something is not working right in your life.

Many different things can cause stress. Physical stress can come when we are afraid of something dangerous. Emotional stress, like worry, can be the result of different issues. **The first step to reducing our stress is to identify what is causing us to be stressed**. What am I stressed about? What is the biggest stress in my life? As a counselor, I help people identify the various things they are stressed about. Lack of money, fear of failure, getting laid off, or failed relationships are all common things that cause stress. Fear and stress walk hand-in-hand.

Scriptures for Learners

Phil 4:4-7 *Rejoice in the Lord always. Again, I will say, rejoice! Let your gentleness be known to all men. The Lord is at hand. Be anxious for nothing, but in everything by prayer and supplication, with thanksgiving, let your requests be made known to God; and the peace of God, which surpasses all understanding, will guard your hearts and minds through Christ Jesus.*

Matthew 11:28-30 *Then Jesus said, "Come to me, all of you who are weary and carry heavy burdens, and I will give you rest. Take my yoke upon you. Let me teach you, because I am humble and gentle at heart, and you will find rest for your souls. For my yoke is easy to bear, and the burden I give you is light."*

Matthew 19:26 *Jesus looked at them intently and said, "Humanly speaking, it is impossible. But with God everything is possible.*

15. Self-management Skills

As we learn to manage ourselves, we are less likely to be annoying to others. Learning self-management skills will help you to be received by people. It is never too late to learn how to live with grace. Saying "please" and "thank you" is a simple way to manage your attitude. When I say "please," it helps me remember that I'm not entitled to the thing I'm asking for. It helps me stay aware that each of us has boundaries. When I ask someone to give me something or to do something for me, I'm asking them to go out of their way a little bit. When I say "please," I acknowledge the other person has value. Saying "please" also helps me remember that the other person has the right to say "no." All kinds of social skills are reinforced in my life when I make it my practice to use the word "please." In the same way when I say "thank you," I am in a practical way exercising an attitude of gratitude. I am giving a gift to the other person and telling them that I appreciate what they have done. Whenever I get a chance to say "thank you," I try to look the person in the eyes. I try to make sure that they understand that what I'm saying is more than just two simple words. I want them to know I genuinely appreciate what they did. (For additional self-management skills, see Appendix G.)

Scriptures for Learners

Colossians 3:12-17 *Since God chose you to be the holy people he loves, you must clothe yourselves with tenderhearted mercy, kindness, humility, gentleness, and patience. Make allowance for each other's faults, and forgive anyone who offends you. Remember, the Lord forgave you, so you must forgive others. Above all, clothe yourselves with love, which binds us all together in perfect harmony. And let the peace that comes from Christ rule in your hearts. For as members of one body you are called to live in peace. And always be thankful. Let the message about Christ, in all its richness, fill your lives. Teach and counsel each other with all the wisdom he gives. Sing psalms and hymns and spiritual songs to God with thankful hearts. And whatever you do or say, do it as a representative of the Lord Jesus, giving thanks through him to God the Father. Let the peace of Christ rule in your hearts, since as members of one body you were called to peace. And be thankful. Let the message of Christ dwell among you richly as you teach and admonish one another with all wisdom through psalms, hymns, and songs from the Spirit, singing to God with gratitude in your hearts. And whatever you do, whether in word or deed, do it all in the name of the Lord Jesus, giving thanks to God the Father through him.*

Colossians 4:5-6 *Live wisely among those who are not believers, and make the most of every opportunity. [6] Let your conversation be gracious and attractive[a] so that you will have the right response for everyone.*

16. The Change Process

God says that we are the light of the world. Even though I don't look like it sometimes, or feel like it, I'm going to say what God says. I'm going to believe God more than I believe what I see, hear, think, or feel. The positive changes take place when I start renewing my mind and when I start thinking the way God does. When I look at myself through God's eyes, change doesn't feel as frightening because I know He loves me so much. If you trade your old cognitive distortions and habits for new positive truth, then change can be very good. It is like trading your old broken down, rusted, ugly car for a brand new one. As you learn more about what is true, and as you practice the life skills, you will change rapidly. An old Chinese proverb says that the journey of a thousand miles starts with a single step. That first step can be really hard if you're thinking about having to walk a thousand miles. The first step is a lot easier if you think about just taking one step at a time.

Take a minute and ask yourself, "What stops me from taking that first step? Is it the fear of failure? Is it the fear of change? Is it a fear of the unknown?"

Sometimes it feels more comfortable to remain stuck than it is to walk into the unknown. When we choose to do things God's way, when we are willing to change so that we get in alignment with Him, the results are amazing. Peace, love, joy, and all the other fruit of the Spirit come as we agree with God and give him control in our lives. Good physical health and abundant life can be ours. Change is challenging but the results are worth it.

Scriptures for Learners

Romans 12:1-2 *And so, dear brothers and sisters, I plead with you to give your bodies to God because of all he has done for you. Let them be a living and holy sacrifice—the kind he will find acceptable. This is truly the way to worship him. Don't copy the behavior and customs of this world,* <u>*but let God transform*</u> *you* <u>*into a new person by changing the way you think.*</u> *Then you will learn to know God's will for you, which is good and pleasing and perfect.*

2 Corinthians 5:17-19 *This means that anyone who belongs to Christ has become a new person. The old life is gone; a new life has begun! And all of this is a gift from God, who brought us back to himself through Christ. And God has given us this task of reconciling people to him. [19] For God was in Christ, reconciling the world to himself, no longer counting people's sins against them. And he gave us this wonderful message of reconciliation.*

17. Free from Codependency

According to Webster's dictionary, codependency can be characterized by denial, low self-esteem, excessive compliance, and/or control patterns. Co-dependent people don't really know who they are or who God created them to be. As a result, they look to other sources or to other people for their value. The enemy doesn't want us to know who we truly are. He wants us to go through life looking to other   people or things for our identity. **God not only knows who you truly are, He can't wait to tell you**. The clearest way to understand yourself is to listen to what God says about who you are. The Bible is full of great promises and statements made by God about each one of us. When we accept Jesus as our Savior, the Holy Spirit comes and lives inside each one of us. His job is to teach us and encourage us. God promised that He will continue the good work that He began in each one of our lives. God's purpose for us is that we grow up to be mature children of the King. God's purpose is that we grow up to look like Jesus.

Codependency causes us to cling to another person. Think about walking with your spouse and holding hands comfortably. Not too loose and not too tight. Codependency would be like clamping down and squeezing the other person's hands so they can't let go. The person who's getting their hand crushed wants to get away and stop the pain.

Scriptures for Learners

Ephesians 3:16-19 *I pray that from his glorious, unlimited resources he will empower you with inner strength through his Spirit. Then Christ will make his home in your hearts as you trust in him. Your roots will grow down into God's love and keep you strong. And may you have the power to understand, as all God's people should, how wide, how long, how high, and how deep his love is. May you experience the love of Christ, though it is too great to understand fully. Then you will be made complete with all the fullness of life and power that comes from God.*

Philippians 1:6 *And I am certain that God, who began the good work within you, will continue his work until it is finally finished on the day when Christ Jesus returns.*

18. Family Roles

We all have a role that we play in our families. A lot of us have grown up in dysfunctional families and we don't even know what role we are playing. Here are some of the common roles people play.

The **scapegoats** are upset with other people because they are blamed for everything. They may act out of a lot of anger. The **victims** are prone to be chemically dependent; they try to go with the flow. Many times they feel powerless. The **family hero** tries to do everything perfectly. He is trying to win the approval of the family. The **lost child** does not feel connected to the family. The **chief enabler** enables the dysfunctional behavior of others in order to feel in control of unmanageable situations and because it is what they are most familiar with. The **mascot** is the family clown; everything is funny. That way they avoid having to look at the problems.

Healthy families do not play unhealthy games. God wants to set us free from all of these unhealthy roles, and he has the power to do it. Of course, the only place to begin is to focus on changing the role that you have been playing.

Key: The root to all of these family roles is control. To release control starts with forgiveness. We need to forgive our families and also to forgive ourselves.

Scriptures for learners

Ephesians 4:11-15 *Now these are the gifts Christ gave to the church: the apostles, the prophets, the evangelists, and the pastors and teachers. Their responsibility is to equip God's people to do his work and build up the church, the body of Christ. This will continue until we all come to such unity in our faith and knowledge of God's Son that we will be mature in the Lord, measuring up to the full and complete standard of Christ. Then we will no longer be immature like children. We won't be tossed and blown about by every wind of new teaching. We will not be influenced when people try to trick us with lies so clever they sound like the truth. Instead, we will speak the truth in love, growing in every way more and more like Christ, who is the head of his body, the church.*

Ephesians 6:1-3 *Children, obey your parents because you belong to the Lord, for this is the right thing to do. "Honor your father and mother." This is the first commandment with a promise: If you honor your father and mother, "things will go well for you, and you will have a long life on the earth."*

19. Developing a Support System

When you are building a support system, you must find people who will hold you accountable and at the same time not shame or discourage you. We all need help, we all need encouragement, and we all need support. **A support system is a group of people that help you with love, encouragement, and accountability**. Dysfunctional families do not have this type of love, encouragement, or accountability. A functional family operates as a support system for the other members of the family. An easy way to tell the difference between a functional family and a dysfunctional family is to determine if you are celebrated or simply tolerated.

God is our main support system, preventing us from the need for codependency. God created us to connect directly with Him. Many people try to plug into other people; at some level, that may work. But, it is not as effective as or as powerful as plugging directly into God. It is like trying to run a dryer, which takes 220 volts, on a 110 volt circuit. The plug doesn't fit correctly and it won't power up the dryer which means the dryer can't do what it has been created to do. When we are plugged into God correctly, we are not tempted to interact with other people in codependent ways. When you are looking for people to be in your support system, you should find people who exhibit good fruit in their lives. Identifying people who have the Fruit of the Spirit in their lives is a good way to find people whom you want to be part of your life

Scriptures for Learners

Acts 20:35 *And I have been a constant example of how you can help those in need by working hard. You should remember the words of the Lord Jesus: 'It is more blessed to give than to receive.'*

Galatians 5:22-25 *But the Holy Spirit produces this kind of fruit in our lives: love, joy, peace, patience, kindness, goodness, faithfulness, gentleness, and self-control. There is no law against these things! Those who belong to Christ Jesus have nailed the passions and desires of their sinful nature to his cross and crucified them there. Since we are living by the Spirit, let us follow the Spirit's leading in every part of our lives.*

Galatians 6:1-2 *Dear brothers and sisters, if another believer is overcome by some sin, you who are godly should gently and humbly help that person back onto the right path. And be careful not to fall into the same temptation yourself. Share each other's burdens, and in this way obey the law of Christ.*

20. Finances

God is serious about our putting Him first in our life. God uses finances to teach us how many different things in the kingdom of God operate. God wants to bless us so that we can be a blessing to other people. All of us want to be blessed financially and I have yet to meet anyone who doesn't. God wants to bless His children as any good father wants to bless his children. The first step to take to get a grasp on your finances is to write down how you have spent your money for the last three months. You cannot control how someone else spends their money, but you can control how you spend yours. Make a decision to honor God with your finances.

You may say, "But Chuck, I can't do that! I don't make enough money to tithe, I always run out of money before the month is over." The first step is often the hardest. Try setting 1% of your income aside for God and ask Him to bless you so you can give more? Your heart attitude when it comes to giving is much more important than the percentage you give. If you stand in a field praying for corn to grow but you haven't planted any corn seed, your prayers won't work. The law of sowing and reaping is not brain surgery. For most people, their billfolds are the last part of them to get saved. God doesn't need your money. The streets of gold in heaven are already paid for. We are the ones who need to freely give our money so we learn that our provision is from God and not from the things our money can buy.

Scriptures for learners

Matt 6:24 *No one can serve two masters. For you will hate one and love the other; you will be devoted to one and despise the other. You cannot serve God and be enslaved to money.*

Malachi 3:10 *"Bring all the tithes into the storehouse so there will be enough food in my Temple. If you do," says the LORD of Heaven's Armies, "I will open the windows of heaven for you. I will pour out a blessing so great you won't have enough room to take it in! Try it! Put me to the test!"*

3 John 2 *Beloved, I pray that you may prosper in all things and be in health, just as your soul prospers.*

21. Breaking the Traps of Anger and Self-hatred

Anger and self-hatred hurt not only the individual but the people around them. It's easy to operate in our flesh. You don't have to take notes about how to do things in a selfish or angry way. We become free from anger and self-hatred by faith as in everything else in the Christian life. If you are offended by someone, what you can say is, "Lord, by faith, I forgive them and I ask you to take this offense out of my heart."

Forgiving someone does not excuse their behavior and it doesn't minimize what they did. It simply puts the responsibility on God to deal with that situation and it takes it off your shoulders. I remember counseling with a rape victim one time and she said, "I hear what you're saying. But what it feels like is that if I forgive him, it's like I'm saying that what he did is okay." I told her that forgiving someone is never saying that what they did is okay. Forgiving someone is saying, "I will not live my life carrying an offense toward you." When we live with un-forgiveness, it is like drinking poison and hoping the other person will die.

If addiction and/or unforgiveness knocks on your door, don't answer. When you carry offense in your heart towards someone else, it can open the door to addictions and self-hatred. God did not create you to carry that burden. A good boundary for you to establish in your life is not to do anything which will contaminate you or someone else.

Scriptures for learners

Matthew 11:28-30 *Then Jesus said, "Come to me, all of you who are weary and carry heavy burdens, and I will give you rest. Take my yoke upon you. Let me teach you, because I am humble and gentle at heart, and you will find rest for your souls. For my yoke is easy to bear, and the burden I give you is light."*

Matthew 22:36-40 *"Teacher, which is the most important commandment in the law of Moses?" Jesus replied, "'You must love the LORD your God with all your heart, all your soul, and all your mind.' This is the first and greatest commandment. A second is equally important: 'Love your neighbor as yourself.' The entire law and all the demands of the prophets are based on these two commandments."*

Ephesians 4:25-27 *So stop telling lies. Let us tell our neighbors the truth, for we are all parts of the same body. And don't sin by letting anger control you. Don't let the sun go down while you are still angry, for anger gives a foothold to the devil.*

22. Becoming a Safe Person

I am not merely talking about physical safety. I am also talking about emotional safety for ourselves and for other people. If we are full of anger and rage, we become an unsafe person for other people and even for ourselves. Galatians 5 discusses the fruits of the flesh and the fruits of the Spirit. The fruits of the flesh will cause us to be unsafe people who are living unsafe lives. What we sow, we will also reap. God also says that sowing to the flesh will repay us a harvest of sin and death. Sowing the things of the Spirit will produce a harvest of love, joy, peace, longsuffering, kindness, goodness, faithfulness, gentleness, and self-control. If I sow unsafe words and deeds into other people's lives, I will reap the same things in my own life. The law of sowing and reaping says you cannot sow wheat and reap corn. There is much drama and trauma in some people's lives. Don't make the mistake of sowing the same kinds of things that they do.

Here are some examples of unsafe and safe people:

Unsafe People	Safe People
Think they have it all together	Admit their weaknesses
Religious – must look good, say the right things	Spiritual, worship God Honest & real in relationship
Defensive	Open to feedback (A wise man loves correction) Prov 8:33
Self-Righteous "I am better than you"	Humble
Apologize (meaning "sorry I got caught")	Humble, repentant Luke 3:8
Demand trust (offended if subjected to any evaluation)	Earn trust (you must watch a person over time/know it takes time)
Lie	Tell the truth
Stagnant	Growing
Blame others	Take responsibility

Scriptures for Learners

John 17:22-23 *I have given them the glory you gave me, so they may be one as we are one. I am in them and you are in me. May they experience such perfect unity that the world will know that you sent me and that you love them as much as you love me.*

Galatians 5:19-23 *When you follow the desires of your sinful nature, the results are very clear: sexual immorality, impurity, lustful pleasures, idolatry, sorcery, hostility, quarreling, jealousy, outbursts of anger, selfish ambition, dissension, division, envy, drunkenness, wild parties, and other sins like these. Let me tell you again, as I have before, that anyone living that sort of life will not inherit the Kingdom of God. But the Holy Spirit produces this kind of fruit in our lives: love, joy, peace, patience, kindness, goodness, faithfulness, gentleness, and self-control. There is no law against these things!*

1 Peter 4:8-10 *Most important of all, continue to show deep love for each other, for love covers a multitude of sins. Cheerfully share your home with those who need a meal or a place to stay. God has given each of you a gift from his great variety of spiritual gifts. Use them well to serve one another.*

23. Changing Your Internal Dialogue

All of us have an internal dialogue. If a person's childhood was full of traumatic events, chances are their internal dialogue is negative. Your internal dialogue is important because it affects how you treat yourself, how you treat other people, and how you think, hope, and dream. If you are feeling much self-hatred, your internal dialogue is probably negative. **People who are hurting will often hurt other people**. Life begins to get exciting when we begin to change our internal dialogue. No one becomes perfect overnight, but things can start to get better very quickly. Hope is like a breath of fresh air. One moment it's not there, the next you feel the breeze on your face.

Scriptures for learners

Proverbs 18:21 *The tongue can bring death or life; those who love to talk will reap the consequences.*

Proverbs 23:7 *For as he thinks in his heart, so is he.*

Matthew 12:33-37 *A tree is identified by its fruit. If a tree is good, its fruit will be good. If a tree is bad, its fruit will be bad. You brood of snakes! How could evil men like you speak what is good and right? For whatever is in your heart determines what you say. A good person produces good things from the treasury of a good heart, and an evil person produces evil things from the treasury of an evil heart. And I tell you this, you must give an account on judgment day for every idle word you speak. The words you say will either acquit you or condemn you.*

24. Parenting Skills

It certainly can be challenging to be a good parent if you have not been parented well. In college, I met a couple who did such a good job as parents. I asked them if they would let me learn from them about how a good family interacts. They used life skills with their kids and I saw the impact on a daily basis. Once, they called in the children from another part of the house because they, as parents, were going to have a conflict. They wanted their kids to learn from it. As they worked through the issue, the children and I were able to observe the speaker/listener technique, conflict resolution, and many other life skills actually used.

A behavioral contract is a helpful tool to use when a child has trouble with appropriate boundaries. It is important for the child to agree to the agreement. Things like chores, bedtime, driving the car, are all important boundaries. **A contract can help the child and parent be on the same page**. There needs to be enforceable and appropriate consequences for the child when the boundaries are broken.

Scriptures for Learners

Proverbs 22:6 *Direct your children onto the right path, and when they are older, they will not leave it.*

Colossians 3:20-21 *Children, always obey your parents, for this pleases the Lord. [21] Fathers, do not aggravate your children, or they will become discouraged.*

James 1:5 *If you need wisdom, ask our generous God, and he will give it to you. He will not rebuke you for asking.*

25. Law of Expectation

The law of expectation is a powerful force that works in many different ways. If you expect to fail, the law of expectation will get you there faster! Another way to think about this is that what we say is what we get. The good news is you can change what you say to yourself. What you say out loud can have a powerful impact on your life and the circumstances around you.

In **Matt 11:24**, Jesus teaches us to speak to the mountain and say, *"Be thou removed." And if you don't doubt in your heart you will have whatever you say.* **Phil 4:19** says, *"I can do all things through Christ who strengthens me."* **We can believe in God's promises to us, or we can believe what we happen to feel like.**

What stops you from living in expectation? Doubt, fear, feeling unworthy, or past failures? We need to treat anything that blocks expectation as a lie and an enemy that we should battle until we have a breakthrough.

God wants us to be like Abraham and say "Amen" to Him even if we don't completely understand how the promise can happen. The key is to study and receive God's great and precious promises and to **renew our minds with His Word.** Every morning we need to declare God's favor over our lives for that day and expect Him to use us for His glory.

Scriptures for Learners

Proverbs 23:7 *For as he thinks in his heart, so is he.*

Mark 11:22-24 *Then Jesus said to the disciples, "Have faith in God. I tell you the truth, you can say to this mountain, 'May you be lifted up and thrown into the sea,' and it will happen. But you must really believe it will happen and have no doubt in your heart. I tell you, you can pray for anything, and if you believe that you've received it, it will be yours.*

Romans 12:2 *Don't copy the behavior and customs of this world, but let God transform you into a new person by changing the way you think. Then you will learn to know God's will for you, which is good and pleasing and perfect.*

Phil 4:13 *For I can do everything through Christ, who gives me strength.*

Appendixes

Appendix A

Time Out

The Time-Out process is a way you can keep yourself from saying or doing things that would damage another person. The following steps are important for you to learn so that you will use Time-Outs correctly.

1. **Are you getting angry?**

   - What is your body saying? (Do you have a headache, faster pulse rate, tense muscles or a tense jaw? Is sweat forming?)

   - What are you saying to yourself? (Our self-talk is very revealing. Are there negative things you're saying to yourself about the other person or about yourself? Are you saying negative things about the situation?)

   - What are you saying out loud? (Name calling and cursing are verbal signs of anger. It's also time for a time-out if you are giving commands to the other person like, "Shut up!" or "Get lost!".)

2. **Take a time-out.** If your clothes catch fire, you should "stop, drop, and roll." That's a good way to think when you take a time-out.

- Stop—Don't try to get the last word in, just say you're taking a time-out and zip your lip.
- Drop—Just drop whatever it is you're talking about or working on and let those things fall out of your hands like a hot potato.
- Roll— Walk yourself right out of the room. I have had to physically grab hold of my tongue at times and walk it out of the room because I wanted to say something so badly.

Discuss how this time-out process works with your spouse before you use it. How long you will be gone and what you will be doing during that period are important things for them to know.

3. **Leave**. (1 hour is a good time frame for a time-out.)
    - Do something physical like walking, running, or cycling.
    - Look at your feelings. (Use "I" statements to help you take responsibility for yourself. "I feel hurt because…"
    - Stand in your partner's shoes. Look at things from their point of view.
    - Do some deep breathing and relaxation exercises.

- Talk to yourself in a positive way. It is a good idea to have a list of Bible-based positive affirmations with you at all times so you can remind yourself of the truth as needed.

4.   **Reconnect.** When you come back from your time-out, ask the other person if now is a good time to talk.

- Take the lead and explain why you felt angry. If you said anything that was unkind, this is a great time to say, "I'm sorry for _____."

- If you become angry again, take another time-out. It's better to take a dozen time-outs than to damage your relationship by saying hurtful things.

- Look for a way so that both of you can win. Your resolution of the situation should be acceptable to both of you.

- If you can't work it out, get some professional help.

Appendix B

Cognitive Distortions

The following is a list of cognitive distortions. If you don't think you have any of these you may be in denial. The truth is that all of us have some or all of the cognitive distortions on this list. Seeing some of the ways you think and act on this list does not mean you are a failure. It simply means you are human, sinful like the rest of us.

1. **All or nothing thinking** is when you look at things in absolute, black and white categories.

2. **Overgeneralization** is viewing a negative event as a never-ending pattern of defeat.

3. **Mental filters** can cause you to dwell on the negative perspectives and ignore the positive ones.

4. **Discounting the positives** is when you insist your accomplishments or positive qualities "don't count."

5. **Jumping to conclusions** is when we decide something is true without evidence to back it up. This could be a result of **Mind reading** which is assuming that people are reacting negatively to us when there is no evidence for it. It could also be **Fortune Telling** which is arbitrarily predicting that things will turn out badly.

6. **Magnification or Minimization** is blowing things way out of proportion or minimizing their importance inappropriately.

7. **Emotional reasoning** is identifying who you are with how you feel. "I feel like an idiot, so I must be one." It could also be letting your feelings control your behavior. "I don't feel like doing this so I will put it off."

8. **"Should" statements** are where you criticize yourself or others with "should" or "should not's." "Musts", "ought", and "have to's" are similar offenders.

9. **Labeling** is identifying with your shortcomings. Instead of saying, "I made a mistake," you tell yourself, "I'm a jerk," "a fool," or "a loser."

10. **Personalization and blame** are when you blame yourself for something you were not entirely responsible for. It can also be blaming others and overlooking the way your own attitudes and behaviors might have contributed to the problem.

These 10 cognitive disorders are adapted from: _Feeling Good: The New Mood Therapy._ Copyright 1980 by David Burns, M.D. (New York: William Borrow and Co. 1980; Signet 1981)

It can be deeply discouraging if you have some of these cognitive distortions. The good news is that you can replace every one of these with truth. Jesus said, _"And you will know the truth and the truth will set you free."_ **(John 8:32)**

Appendix C

Cognitive Distortion Worksheet

How do we get out of these negative ways of thinking? Cognitive distortions can be tricky and a bit sneaky. Just when you identify one, another one pops up. Then, after a while, the first one seems to come back after you thought you had defeated it. Don't forget that all of us are in process. We don't practice so that we can be perfect; we practice to get better.

The following form will help you identify some of the cognitive distortions that you may have. The easiest way to identify them is when you find yourself behaving badly! The reason to use this kind of worksheet is to get to the truth.

For example: I'm driving and it's a great day. Suddenly someone in a little Porsche cuts in front of me and makes me slam on my brakes. A pebble from their tire hits my windshield and I see a starburst form. I have gone immediately from having a great day, enjoying everything and praising the Lord, to anger. I'm driving so I can't stop and fill out a form but when I get home this form can help me process what made me so angry. It takes no effort at all to stay in the angry mindset. The work comes as we examine our thoughts and feelings and then take steps to come out of those bad habits.

Cognitive Distortion Worksheet

1. **EVENT--What happened?** Briefly describe the event

2. **UNCOMFORTABLE EMOTION--How do you feel about it?** This could simply be anger. As you practice doing this kind of exercise, you may find that under the anger are some other feelings like hurt or frustration.

3. **NEGATIVE THOUGHTS—Identify them word for word.** What are you thinking about what just occurred?

4. **DIAGNOSE THOUGHTS—examine your thoughts** using the list of cognitive distortions at the bottom of the page.

5. **REALISTIC THOUGHTS—Use the four guidelines** at the bottom of the page to help you establish new thoughts about the event.

Cognitive Distortions: 1) All or nothing thinking; 2) Over-generalization: 3) Mental Filter; 4) Discounting the positive; 5) Jumping to conclusions (mind reading/fortune telling); 6) Magnification; 7) Emotional reasoning; 8) "Shoulds"; 9) Labeling; 10) Blame.

Realistic Thoughts: 1) Answer/address the negative thought;

2) Answer without using cognitive distortions;

3) Be believable to "me";

4) Use "I" messages.

When I get down to the realistic thought part of this process, I begin by giving the other person the benefit of the doubt. It may take a few minutes to go through the first few stages because when we are upset, blood flows away from our brain. I begin to imagine what might have caused that person's irrational behavior.

"He may have gotten a call that his kids are hurt, or perhaps his wife was taken into the emergency room. He's just trying to get there as fast as he can. He wasn't aiming that rock to hit my windshield; that's just a road hazard."

Even after I go through this process and have some reasonable explanations for his bad behavior, I might be tempted to stop midway and say, "No, he's just a jerk!" Suddenly, I'm back at the beginning and have to repeat the entire process!

The Bible says in Galatians 5 that we naturally love to do the wrong things; that is our nature. We break that evil way of thinking by focusing on realistic thoughts and yielding ourselves to the ways of God. That is what places the flesh under subjection and that is what places our negative thinking under subjection. We really do have power over our thoughts. Many things in our lives are beyond our control. But we can control what we think about, and that is good news.

The more you practice giving people the **benefit** of the doubt and not the doubt, a new, good habit will be formed in you. It takes 20-30 days to form a habit; so, don't try this for only a day or two. Keep doing it over and over so that it becomes a part of your life. The more we practice something, the better we get at it.

Use this sheet for anything that happens in your life. At work, with family, even events from the past. "Bless those that curse you and pray for those who hurt you."

"Why should I do that? I don't even like them!" you may be thinking. The answer is simple. You need to practice praying, and they need the prayer.

Appendix D

The Speaker/listener technique

As the speaker:

    1. Speak for yourself. Don't try to read the other persons mind or expect them to read yours.

    2. Use "I" messages. It is not selfish or self-centered in a conversation to tell the other person how you feel.

    3. Don't bring up the "kitchen sink." Stick to one issue. Don't bring up the past.

    4. Don't use words such as, "Always or never." Those are conclusive words. They convey the message that you know all the information.

    5. Use words like, "It seems like," or, "It feels like." These phrases open the door for the other person to give you information.

    6. Take a "time-out" if anger escalates.

    7. Edit your thoughts before you say them. The way to do this is to actually say them over in your mind before you speak them out loud.

    8. Don't talk incessantly. If you do, you are likely to wear people out. That doesn't resolve the issue; it merely buries it.

As the listener:

1. Paraphrase or mirror back what you hear. Your purpose is to let the speaker know you definitely understand. These phrases will help you in this process.

- "What I hear you saying is..."
- "Is it correct, then, to say..."
- "So it sounds like..."
- "It seems that you think..."
- "As I understand then..."

2. Focus on the speaker's message. Don't try to correct them or add your own perspective. This is not easy; this will take practice. You will hear the speaker say things that are not accurate and you will want to correct them. "Oh, no, no, no, no, no! It was not like that at all..." you may be thinking. Wait your turn! You can explain your feelings and what you perceived happening when it's your turn to be the speaker.

3. Ask questions that help the speaker share more deeply. Questions that invite more sharing:

a. Tell me more about that.

b. On a scale of 1-10, how much did it impact you?

c. What about that bothers you?

Your purpose as the listener is to empathize. Empathy is a choice. This is not problem-solving. The goal is to hear each other and understand the other person's feelings. We all just want to be heard and validated.

Why should you listen? The other person may know things that you don't. Their perspective is vital for fuller understanding. It shows respect and value.

Appendix E

Identity Exercise from Psalm 139

This is how God thinks about you. Insert your name in the Psalm and let the Holy Spirit give you a glimpse of how precious you are. God obviously wanted you to be born, as evidenced by this passage.

Many people believe they were a mistake because their parents conveyed that they were an accident. "I didn't plan to have you." That is heard by a child as, "I'm a mistake," or, "I was an accident," or, "I'm not wanted or loved."

Psalm 139

O LORD, you have examined my heart and know everything about me. You know when I sit down or stand up. You know my thoughts even when I'm far away. You see me when I travel and when I rest at home. You know everything I do. You know what I am going to say even before I say it, LORD. You go before me and follow me. You place your hand of blessing on my head. Such knowledge is too wonderful for me, too great for me to understand! I can never escape from your Spirit! I can never get away from your presence! If I go up to heaven, you are there; if I go down to the grave, you are there. If I ride the wings of the morning, if I dwell by the farthest oceans, even there your hand will guide me, and your strength will support me. I could ask the darkness to hide me and the light around me to become night—

but even in darkness I cannot hide from you. To you the night shines as bright as day. Darkness and light are the same to you. You made all the delicate, inner parts of my body and knit me together in my mother's womb. Thank you for making me so wonderfully complex! Your workmanship is marvelous—how well I know it. You watched me as I was being formed in utter seclusion, as I was woven together in the dark of the womb. You saw me before I was born. Every day of my life was recorded in your book. Every moment was laid out before a single day had passed. How precious are your thoughts about me, O God. They cannot be numbered! I can't even count them; they outnumber the grains of sand! And when I wake up, you are still with me! O God, if only you would destroy the wicked! Get out of my life, you murderers! They blaspheme you; your enemies misuse your name. O LORD, shouldn't I hate those who hate you? Shouldn't I despise those who oppose you? Yes, I hate them with total hatred, for your enemies are my enemies. Search me, O God, and know my heart; test me and know my anxious thoughts. Point out anything in me that offends you, and lead me along the path of everlasting life.

Appendix F

Adult strategies

Ventilation: Everyone needs a constructive way to release pent-up emotion. When we are angry, over thirty different chemicals are released in our bodies which give us a great deal of energy. Recognize that energy and find a positive release. Do something physical. Do not harm yourself or others. Exercise helps you reacclimatize the adrenaline back into your system. Adrenaline flows when you escalate and it takes time for it to blend into your system again.

Active listening: This helps us be certain that we understand what the other person is saying.

Apologize: Saying "I'm sorry" is a choice you can make. if you're wrong about something, you can always own your mistake and apologize. Be empathetic. The Bible says in Proverbs 15:1, "A soft answer turns away wrath." It is much more difficult to be angry with someone who is empathetic and who is using a soft, kind voice.

Postponement: Individually agree to wait for a more appropriate time to discuss the situation, allowing tempers to cool. Take a time out and check back in with them after one hour to see if they are ready to talk. Postponement should not be more than a few hours.

Humor: Laughter is a great stress reliever. The Bible says a cheerful heart is healthy for you to have. Put-downs and sarcasm are destructive. They are out of bounds, even if they may seem funny to you.

Compromise: Each person gives up something and also gains something in a compromise situation so that the issues can be resolved. Look for the highest common truth and not the lowest common denominator.

Explain without threatening: Keep the conflict centered on the issue. Separating the deed from the doer. Threats can also include the fear of rejection by the other. Rejection of them as a person as well as rejection of their idea. An "I-message" expresses feelings and needs without judgment. The *child* position wants to have its own way all the time and does not want to explain. When we interact from the *adult* position, we are explaining the situation and our feelings about the situation.

Brainstorm: Using your creativity, come up with ten to twelve ways to resolve the conflict. A few will be mutually acceptable and work well. The ability to think beyond the first idea that comes into your head is a very important life skill. We want to find a win-win solution.

Reduction: Reduce things into manageable parts, then deal with them one at a time. It is so easy in a conflict situation for us to jump around to a number of topics without closing out the first topic. The *child* doesn't know how to resolve conflicts because it is not teachable. Put boundaries on the conflict and find areas of agreement and disagreement.

Writing: Writing helps you clarify your thoughts and feelings. It is also a good way to vent some volatile emotions without contaminating the relationship. Start with the words "I feel," "I want," "I need." After negotiating an agreement, when you plan to follow-through, write down who will do what, when, and for how long?

Fact-finding: When you learn to live in the *adult* position, you will not tolerate gossip. You cannot always prevent it, but you don't have to be party to it. Try to obtain all the relevant facts and feelings.

Role-playing: This is looking at the problem from the other person's point of view. It is like walking in their shoes.

Third-party intervention: You might have to have a counselor or a pastor sit down with you and the other person to talk with them. A third party is also important if you think you might be in harm's way while talking with them. Make sure the person is truly neutral and is not biased toward one person or the other.

In **First Corinthians 13**, Paul stated that he put away childish things. He didn't ask God to do it, he did it himself. These *adult* strategies help us put away childish things when we communicate with each other.

Appendix G

Self-Management Skills

1. Say "please" and "thank you".

2. Choose to be professional no matter who you are with.

3. Walk in integrity and loyalty.

4. Don't hold on to offenses.

5. Don't exploit other people's personal flaws.

6. Avoid the gossip trap. (1 Timothy 5:13)

7. Balance grace with truth.

8. Don't assume that you know what people need. Ask them to tell you what they need.

9. Resist dominating the conversation.

10. Ask the question, "Can you tell me one thing I did that hurt you this week?

11. We teach people how to treat us. If you live your life as a martyr, you will not be able to live a healthy life or have healthy relationships.

12. Take care of yourself by: getting enough sleep; eating healthy food; drinking enough water; and exercising. If you don't take care of the simple physical things, you're going to need a miracle from God every day just to feel normal.

13. Get regular physical checkups. This includes dental checkups and eye exams.

14. Keep the flesh under subjection. (Galatians 5)

15. Manage your emotions. (Philippians 2:5)

16. Take every thought captive. (2 Corinthians 10:5)

17. Live your life under submission to God and others. (Ephesians 5:21)

18. Do not live in fear. (2 Timothy 1:7)

19. Seek God's approval, not man's.

About Chuck...

Physically and emotionally broken at birth, Chuck Lewis was not expected to live. As God began healing his body over those first few years, he remained emotionally, even spiritually, broken.

Everything changed for Chuck at sixteen when he asked and accepted Jesus into his heart. Everything changed again in his twenties when he was hit by a drunk driver and sustained another spinal cord injury.

Chuck's story will make you laugh and it will make you cry. But it will also give you hope.

"A Broken Candle Still Gives Light" is the Chuck Lewis Story

Made in the USA
Coppell, TX
08 January 2023

10693323R00111